To
Nauman
with
May
thaks
for
taking
Care
of
us

Ziv ben Shimon H.Gvi:
Alio
Wann Kouton

Spring 2015

Introduction to
The World of Kabbalah

By the same author:

Adam & The Kabbalistic Trees
A Kabbalistic Universe
The Way of Kabbalah
The Kabbalist at Work
Kabbalah and Exodus
Kabbalah: School of the Soul
Psychology and Kabbalah
The Kabbalistic Tree of Life
Kabbalah & Astrology
The Anointed–*a Kabbalistic novel*
Anatomy of Fate
The Path of a Kabbalist
A Kabbalistic View of History

By Other Publishers:

Kabbalah—The Divine Plan (*HarperCollins*)
Kabbalah, Tradition of Hidden Knowledge (*Thames & Hudson*)
Astrology, The Celestial Mirror (*Thames & Hudson*)
As Above So Below (*Stuart & Watkins*)

For
Azriel of Gerona
Innovator and Consolidator

Also for
Patricia Buckle
a memorial

Introduction to
The World of Kabbalah

Z'ev ben Shimon Halevi

Bet El Trust
Registered Charity No. 288712

www.kabbalahsociety.org
E-mail: books@kabbalahsociety.org

First published in 2008 by Kabbalah Society
Copyright © Z'ev ben Shimon Halevi 2008

*The illustrations on pages 28, 32, 102, 118, 157, 190 and 216 are
reproduced by kind permission of Dover Publications Inc.*

A CIP catalogue record for this book
is available from the British Library.

ISBN 13: 978-1-909171-04-6

Printed and bound by Lightning Source UK Ltd., Milton Keynes

Design by Tree of Life Publishing
www.treeoflifepublishing.co.uk

Contents

Illustrations

FIGURE 1.—JACOB'S LADDER
This is Kabbalah's metaphysical and mythological picture of Existence. At the
top are the words 'NO-THING-NESS' and 'LIMITLESSNESS' which define the
Absolute. Below comes the first manifestation of Existence in the primordial Tree
of Life and its ten Divine principles. These govern the three lower Worlds of
Creation, Formation and Action. Within this relative frame of different realities
are various orders of creatures. Humanity, however, has its origin in the highest
Universe of Azilut or Emanation. (Watercolour by James Russell, 20th century.)

Preface

Kabbalah is the esoteric dimension of Judaism. It dates back to Abraham and beyond. Over time, it has undergone many changes of form, according to the needs of history, but it has always been essentially the same. Behind the accumulation of various practices, elaborate symbolism and complex metaphysics is the Torah or Teaching about the relationship between God, the universe and humanity. Kabbalah deals with the origin and purpose of Existence and the objective of the Absolute in the drama of Creation. What follows is an outline of the tradition as seen in a combination of ancient, medieval and modern viewpoints. Out of this will emerge, it is hoped, a clearer picture of what has become obscure over the centuries. The Divine Plan is self-evident once its principles are seen and acted upon.

Z'ev ben Shimon Halevi
Autumn 5766/2006
London

Figure 2—ABRAHAM AND MELCHIZEDEK
This is where the Tradition begins. Here the mysterious Righteous King who had neither father nor mother, indicating he was a supernatural being, initiates Abraham who was seeking to find the Absolute who generated and ruled Existence. The bread and wine given to him represent the theory and practice of esoteric knowledge that can lead to direct experience of the Divine and its purpose. (Austrian altar piece by Nicholas of Verdun, 12th century.)

Introduction

The origin of Kabbalah traditionally goes back to Abraham who was initiated into *Hockmah Nestorah*—the "Hidden Wisdom"—by Melchizedek around four thousand years ago. It is, in reality, much older, going back into prehistory. Kabbalah is the Jewish medieval name for the esoteric Teaching that is to be found at the heart of every spiritual tradition, be it primitive or of the most sophisticated kind, providing that line is still a genuine source of mystical experience and knowledge.

Kabbalah, although it was not always known by that name, has been evolving over many centuries, adapting its terms to the religious and philosophical language of various times and places. Today it not only uses ancient and medieval frames of reference but modern scientific and psychological terms to illuminate the eternal principles. This is why it has endured the passage of history and the impact of many cultures. However, the basic scheme is always the same although it may use symbolism, metaphysics or even a physical example to explain the workings of the Divine plan.

The purpose of Existence, according to Kabbalah, is that God wishes to behold God in the process of the universe's evolution and the Self realisation of humanity which is the instrument by which such an event can come about. This book is aimed to hint at why you, the reader, are here on Earth, who you truly are and what your part and destiny might be in this cosmic drama.

Figure 3—MOSES ON MOUNT SINAI
Here the Torah, or Teaching, that was almost lost is given again. Moses, in this
image, is in the high state of enlightenment, symbolised by the top of the mountain.
Below, the Children of Israel, that is those who are still young souls, wait to
receive instruction from the House of Israel or those older souls who are mature
enough to understand what Moses will teach. They are known as the elders and
chiefs of the twelve tribes that represent all humanity. (Bank's Bible, 19th century.)

1. Origins

The term Kabbalah was first used in medieval Spain by Solomon Ibn Gabirol, an 11th century Spanish Jewish philosopher, poet and mystic. This Hebrew word has several meanings. Its essence is to be 'receptive' or 'to receive' which can be understood in different ways. The historic view is that this tradition of esoteric knowledge was passed on by word of mouth or written down for each generation. That is the horizontal line. The other is the vertical. By this is meant that which has been received by direct mystical experience. While one may study old Kabbalistic texts they are, in reality, not source material, even though they were written by mystics, as there is a vast experiential gap between reading about the higher realms and actually entering them.

In earlier times, Jewish mystics were known by various names. Some were called 'Those who know the field', meaning Existence. Others were termed 'Riders of the Chariot', that is, those who attained the prophetic level of vision of Ezekiel and beheld the higher worlds symbolised by the image of a vast Chariot, Throne and Fiery Man which represented the three upper cosmoses. Yet others were called those who 'Go down into the Chariot', that is, delved into the depths of themselves and viewed the microcosm of a human being which is a miniature and interior image of Existence. Yet others were simply called 'Those who know', the implication being that they were intensely conscious of both the outer and inner, invisible realities.

This difference is set out in the Book of Exodus. Here there are those named 'The Children of Israel' in contrast to those called 'The House of Israel'. By this definition, the as-yet young souls are differentiated from the more mature souls, represented by the tribal leaders and Levite priesthood, who understand the deeper meaning of the Teaching or Torah. This esoteric and exoteric difference is symbolised by the two tablets that Moses brought down from Mount Sinai. One tablet was to be studied and practiced by day, meaning to be presented to the multitude in its most obvious form; and the other

16

Figure 4—EZEKIEL'S VISION
When the first Temple was destroyed and the Judeans were exiled to Babylon, the
Teaching had to take on a new form. Here the doctrine of the Four Worlds that
make up Existence are cast in the form of the elements of the Earth; the Chariot of
Formation and its various wheeled cycles; the spiritual Throne of Heaven and the
Fiery Man who represents Adam Kadmon, the Divine image of God, composed of
pure Light. This metaphoric model of Existence was studied in a deep mystical
state by experienced individuals trained in the discipline of a school of the soul.
This meant the Torah could survive without the Temple or being in Jerusalem. Here
began the esoteric tradition of the Jewish Diaspora. (Bear Bible, 17th century.)

to be discreetly contemplated and acted upon at night, by initiates, in secret so as to discover the esoteric or hidden mystical content of the Torah.

According to tradition, the Bible has four levels at which it can be comprehended. The lowest level of understanding is the literal; the second the symbolic; the third, the metaphysical and the highest, direct mystical experience. Kabbalah takes into account all these levels as each has its contribution to make as regards the aim of Existence, the purpose of humanity and its relation to the Deity.

The Bible begins with the story of Creation. This, according to the Kabbalah, is the second stage of manifestation. The first, as indicated by the originally oral teaching, begins with the emergence of space out of NO-THING-NESS. This is accomplished by the Absolute withdrawing into ITSELF in order to allow Existence to come into being. Into this void were emanated ten Divine Numbers or sefirot and twenty-two Hebrew letters that represented the major and minor laws that were to govern all the worlds and their inhabitants. After this primordial Divine Realm filled space, the spiritual level of Creation then emerged. The Seven Days of Creation are described by the written tradition of the Bible as a cosmic process in which Fire, symbolised by Light, and the other three elements of Air, Water and Earth are organised into an ordered cosmos in which three different levels of creatures can exist. At this point all are still spiritual essences. Then comes the world of Formation or Eden, followed by the material domain of Action.

The stories of Adam and Eve in the Garden of Eden are mythological; that is they describe, in poetic form, important events prior to humanity's descent into matter. This is a clear statement that mankind pre-existed its terrestrial form. There are many legends in every folk tradition that give insights into humanity's relationship with the non-physical, invisible Higher Worlds, life after death, gods and demons and spiritual evolution. The Bible does the same but it is largely hidden within the text. The key to this is set out in the early chapters of the Book of Genesis. In the story of the *Nephilim*, the 'fallen ones', these highly evolved humans, 'the Sons of God', mated with the 'daughters of men'; that is, as-yet unevolved souls. The result was a tribe of intelligent but violent people who ravished the Earth and humanity. Knowledge is power and must therefore not be given to those who are not yet responsible, lest they abuse it. This is why Kabbalah has always been a discreet tradition.

Figure 5—CREATION
The six Days of Creation unfold according to a definite sequence. First, light or Fire comes into being, followed by the firmament or Air and then Water and Earth with plants, the first manifestation of life. Then comes the ordering of the cosmos from the galaxy to the atom. Into this spiritual universe are brought the Fowl of the Air or archangels; the Fish of the Sea or angels who will inhabit the watery world of Formation; and finally the Beasts of the Field or Earthly organic creatures. Adam and humanity appear on the sixth Day and are, according to Kabbalah, a second spiritual manifestation of the Divine Fiery, primordial Adam Kadmon. (Bank's Bible, 19th century.)

Another example is the building of the Tower of Babel when the collective mind of a civilisation believed it could challenge God and invade Heaven. The result was confusion for, when esoteric ideas are misunderstood and misused by the ignorant, their meanings are distorted. This is also why the great Flood occurred. Then the level of human corruption was so great that it had to be all but destroyed. However, the Teaching was preserved in the symbol of the Ark whose design is seen by Kabbalists as being based upon the diagram of Jacob's Ladder. In this metaphysical scheme, each triangle is the home of different pairs of animals who represented various branches of knowledge. The oriental image of Shangri-La, a place to preserve civilisation in times of destruction, is a parallel legend.

With the story of Abram, there is a shift from myth and legend to history. From here on, the Bible weaves esoteric principles with actual events. Abram came from the identifiable city of Ur in what is now Iraq. The ruins of this trade, industrial and cultural centre can still be seen. This was to be the setting of the Bible's first flesh-and-blood character. In Jewish folklore, Abram is no ignorant desert wanderer but a well-educated urban man who did not believe in the idols his father sold in his shop. There must be, Abram concluded after studying the array of Mesopotamian gods, an Absolute Deity who governed the whole of Existence. Stimulated by a visionary dream in which he is told to go to a distant country, he sets out to discover the Ultimate. This symbolises the first step of a very long spiritual search. As with many seekers, he searches in vain in far away places, only to realise the journey is not horizontal but vertical. When this realisation occurs, he meets Melchizedek, 'the Righteous King', near the site of the future Jerusalem. For the Kabbalist, this critical encounter represents the synchronicity of an external event and a particular point of development. When such a moment comes, it signifies that an individual is ready for an initiation into what is called the Way or Path by many spiritual traditions.

Melchizedek, during a ceremony that awakens Abram's soul, gives him wine and bread. These are symbols of the theory and practice of the Teaching. They represent the two outer pillars of the Tree of Life diagram, to be explained further on. They are also to be recognised in the Rod and Staff of the Book of Exodus. The middle column of the Tree is the Path up the Holy Mountain and to the Promised Land.

According to legend, Melchizedek had neither father nor mother, indicating he was a supernatural being. He was, according to

Figure 6—NOAH'S ARK
This is a symbol of the preservation of the Teaching during disastrous periods in history. The design of the boat can be seen in the structure of Jacob's Ladder. Each of the triads that compose it is a chamber for a particular pair of creatures, representing different aspects of theory and practice, from the lowest to the highest level. Noah's name means "Rest," to be secure and safe, while the wickedness of an epoch destroys itself. It is an early example of Shangri-La, a place to preserve civilisation while destruction is going on in the world. (Bank's Bible, 19th century.)

Kabbalah, originally known as Enoch whose name means 'the Initiate'. In the Bible, Enoch was the only righteous man of an earlier and wicked generation. To avoid contact with this evil society, Enoch would spend much time alone in deep meditation. While on one of these interior excursions he was taken up, out of the body, and shown the Higher Worlds and their inhabitants. The whole of the history of humanity was revealed to him in the image of a vast curtain hanging down before Heaven. In this, each thread represented a soul and its length the journey of destiny through Time. After experiencing this and other visions, Enoch was instructed to found the first School of the Soul, to which the kings of the Earth would come to be spiritually educated. The monarchs represented the most advanced individuals of the period. When they completed their training these masters returned, each to their own land, to found a local esoteric tradition. Many ancient cultures refer to a mysterious founder who strongly resembles Enoch. Thoth of Egypt, the first spiritual emperor of China and the mythical Greek, Hermes Trismegistus, are examples.

When Enoch's mission on Earth was complete he was taken up into Heaven, without going through the process of death, and transfigured into a human archangelic being called Metatron. As such, Enoch/ Metatron was the first fully Self-realised individual. In Abram's case he appeared as Melchizedek but later he manifested as Elijah. In Jewish folklore he takes on the form of a miracle-working old man or a young boy and even a courtesan, in order to instruct or protect an initiate. After being given the secrets of Existence, Abram was renamed Abraham, 'Father of many people'. By this is meant that he would be the source of many Schools of the Soul. This indeed came to pass, as seen in the three monotheistic religions and many other spiritual lines in the world.

Initially, the purely Abrahamic version of the Teaching was passed on to his son, Isaac. It then came to Jacob before being transmitted to Levi, one of his sons. Moses was born into the tribe of Levi. After the Mount Sinai revelation, the Teaching was given to the new priesthood. Later the Judges and Prophets were the vehicles of the Tradition. With the destruction of the second Temple in the Roman period, the hidden aspect of the Torah was preserved by the more mystical rabbis. They passed it on over many centuries, changing its outer form to suit each time and place without altering its inner content. This was done by weaving the Teaching into rituals, prayers and rabbinic metaphysics. Needless to say, over time outdated forms were reduced to the level

Figure 7—ENOCH

This name means the "Initiate." He was the only righteous person in a dark age of human history. Retiring from an evil society, he went deep into himself and so rose above physical limitations. During these meditations, he was taken into the upper Worlds to see the structure, processes and inhabitants of Paradise and Heaven. During one spiritual excursion, he was lifted into the highest and Divine realm and shown secrets of which even the archangels had no knowledge. Upon returning to Earth, he founded the first school of the soul. (Manuscript, 11th century.)

of religious superstition by those who did not understand what certain rituals, symbols and ideas actually meant. This led to an increasing accumulation of unintelligible material that obscured the Teaching of the mystical line. For example, the significance of the twelve tribes was lost. They represent the twelve types of soul that make up humanity. This originated in Mesopotamia where Abraham, who was familiar with astrology as a study of the psyche and its destiny, came from. He, however, knew that the Sun, Moon and planetary gods were just angelic servants of the Absolute and not the ultimate arbiters of fate. This view was later all but forgotten or rejected by rabbinic scholars who only understood the letter of the law. Fortunately, in the Middle Ages, the astrological connection was revived by such mystical poets and philosophers as Ibn Gabirol and Ibn Ezra and developed by the Jewish intelligentsia, despite the objection of the great scholar, Maimonides, who admitted he was no mystic.

By the medieval period, the esoteric aspect of the Teaching was spread far and wide among the Jews of the diaspora who had evolved many different forms of Kabbalah, as the inner Teaching was now called. However, all drew upon a central core based upon the Bible, especially the first chapter of Genesis. To these were added many myths and legends, not included in the Biblical canon, which deepened the understanding of the text.

Figure 8—METATRON
At the end of his mission Enoch was transformed, without going through the
process of death, to the highest level of Heaven to be transfigured into Metatron
who would fill the place vacated by Lucifer when it rebelled against God. As a
human with archangelic powers, Enoch is a master of time and space. He can go
anywhere and enter any period to aid and instruct worthy individuals. To
Abraham, he appeared as Melchizedek; later as Elijah. In other cultures he is
known as Thoth, Hermes Trismegistus and Fu Hsi, the Teacher of teachers.
(Byzantine, 13th century.)

2. *Mythology*

The religious and philosophical language of the ancient world was mythology. The Fall or, to be more accurate, the Descent from Eden, is a fine example. The Bible tells us how Adam was brought forth on the Sixth Day of Creation with the significant comment that 'they' were created 'In the image of God', male and female. By this was meant that the 'spiritual' Adam was a composite entity. Eve, the feminine principle, was later separated from the side of Adam. This occurred at the level of the third World of Formation called, in Genesis, the Garden of Eden. This is the realm of the soul. Eve was to be Adam's psychological complement or soul mate. This event indicates that there were now three distinct universes; that is the Divine realm and the dimensions of Spirit and Soul. These different realities are seen in the symbols of the Divine Tree of Life and the Spiritual Tree of Knowledge above and within Paradise. The fourth and lowest world of Action was brought into being on the Sixth Day of Creation but it is, at this point, as yet only a creative idea. The material realm only fully manifested later in form and matter, after the Big Bang brought the physical universe into being.

The Oral version of Genesis contains many other interesting esoteric concepts. For example, according to one legend, Adam had a wife before Eve. She was Lilith who wanted to acquire Adam's masculine powers. The Creator declined to offset the sexual balance of humanity and so Lilith, having free will, left Adam and became the spouse of Asmodeus, the King of the Demons, whom she could manipulate. When Eve was brought in as a substitute to be the feminine factor, Lilith became jealous of Eve and continually seeks to destroy her children. This can occur at birth or in life through seduction. In every culture there are stories that illustrate how cosmic laws can be abused and disrupt the scheme of Creation. Prometheus stealing the fire, or knowledge, from Heaven is but one example. This led to the making of metal weapons and war. However, the 'fall' of Adam and Eve is not, when seen from a Kabbalistic viewpoint, quite the severe

Figure 9—HEAVENS
This illumination is based upon the vision of Hildegard of Bingen, a medieval mystic. She saw with her mind's eye the archangels of the stars and the four elements. This image represents what Plato called the World of Ideas. This is the realm of essences or spirit of things before they become forms and later manifest in the material world. This same process is seen at the human level in the conception of a work of art, before it is designed and made. The physical universe is, in reality, but a figment of the Holy One's imagination because beneath the subatomic realm there is the void of No-Thing-Ness. (Illumination of Hildegard of Bingen, 12th century.)

Figure 10—THE SPIRITUAL ADAM
This image of God is the second manifestation of the reflection of the Absolute.
Like the Divine Adam Kadmon, this Adam is both male and female. This description
is set out in the Book of Genesis which is the written portion of the Kabbalistic
tradition. That which is concerned with the Divine realm belongs to the oral line
that runs parallel but behind the written word. Here we see YAHVEH ELOHIM
in the role of Creator bringing Adam into being in the first of the three lower
Worlds of separation. Because of this step away from the perfection of the Divine
realm, imperfection or evil can occur, symbolised by the snake. (William Blake,
19th century.)

Figure 11—LUCIFER'S REBELLION
This occurred at the only time that the angelic host had free will. This temporary gift was to be exercised in a judgement as to which was the superior in rank; Lucifer, the highest archangel or the second Adam who appeared on the sixth Day of Creation. While Adam, the most complete image of God, was creative, Lucifer had no imagination in the context of naming the animals. Lucifer was humiliated before all the angelic host and left Heaven with a third of them who chose to follow their champion. They became the demonics led by Lucifer, now renamed Satan the Tester, who envied humanity and would seek to stop all development. (Doré's Illustrations for Milton's *Paradise Lost*, 19th century)

sentence for sin as it seems but a Divine 'set up'. Adam and Eve could do what they liked except eat of the Tree of Knowledge and what they did was not unexpected. Moreover, it is clear that the Holy One knew exactly how Lucifer would react. A wise and omniscient parent can easily design a plot in which the children will produce an inevitable result, so as to define a role which each will perform to perfection. Let us consider the Biblical myth.

The angelics preceded Adam. They are the birds who inhabit the upper airy World of Creation; and the fish, or angels, of the sea who exist in the lower watery World of Formation. Lucifer, the highest Archangel was, however, somewhat affronted by the arrival of Adam on the Sixth Day. As the 'Bearer of the Light' how could this late-comer take precedence over it, the head of all the angelics? The Creator, anticipating this reaction, therefore arranged for a contest to take place, before the whole Heavenly Host, between Adam and Lucifer to decide who had the greater power. In this, each contestant was required to give a name to each Beast of the Field as these archetypes of every species that was to appear on the Earth had, as yet, no titles. To add spice to the contest, the Creator declared that on that Day, each angelic could choose whom they would support. This was the one time the angels would be allowed to go beyond their cosmic function and exercise free will.

Lucifer, full of pride, accepted the challenge believing it could easily outwit this human contender for the prime position in the universe. As each animal was brought forth, Adam had no problem naming them because he, as the most complete image of God, had the gift of creativity while Lucifer could not conjure up a single syllable because it did not have this creativity. Only humanity had this capacity. Adam's abundant flow of new and witty offerings, in contrast to Lucifer's silence, revealed that Lucifer was no more than a brilliant, cosmic civil servant who knew all the rules but had no imagination. Lucifer was thus humiliated before the whole celestial company. Those angelics who supported Lucifer were outraged. The result was that a third of the Heavenly Host suddenly rebelled and departed Heaven with their leader, railing against God as they retreated into the depths and extreme edges of Existence. Thus, by their own choice, they became the host of demons.

The Holy One set up this situation because a cosmic destructive factor was needed to destroy corruption, degradation and waste within Existence. The rebellious angelics thus had voluntarily chosen their

30

Figure 12—GOOD AND EVIL
The processes of creation and destruction, and of good and evil, are vital to the progression of Existence, from primordial innocence to fully mature experience. Without death there cannot be birth; and without testings, no evolution. This is seen throughout life, the microcosm of the macrocosm. Good and evil are about moral issues rather than physical phenomena. At the human level, anyone can appear to be saintly until they are tested. The choice as to which side one chooses is crucial in development. Without temptation and sin, there can be no reward or punishment; two vital factors in human evolution. (Dürer, 16th century)

grim positions. The role of Lucifer, now called Satan the Tester, was to oppose humanity so as to test its integrity. This was vital for human evolution; for without resistance, challenges and opposition, Adam and Eve could not find out what they were and were not meant to do. Satan is the Dark principle that can arise within an individual or community. All who are tempted to go against Divine Law will find that there are dire consequences that force them back onto the path of Evolution. This is the reason for Evil. The first commandment was not to eat of the Tree of Knowledge. From this, the human couple learnt about karma, called in Kabbalah 'Measure for Measure'. The Holy One knew exactly what Adam and Eve would do and how Lucifer and some angels would respond. They all had no-one to blame except themselves. In Hebrew, the word *Het* or Sin means 'to miss the mark'. It is not quite as damning as some zealous clergy make out. There is always the possibility of correction or salvation, if remorse is experienced in the acknowledgement of error. Thus the Fall was not quite the disaster it appears to be. Moreover, how else could the Holy One ease Adam and Eve out of the pleasant domain of Paradise and down into the physical realm and get Lucifer to take on the role of Satan? Here began the great journey of human evolution as individuals slowly Self-realised the Divine spark within themselves.

The highest Holy Name is I AM THAT I AM. In this utterance that generated Existence, this Title or WORD will be echoed in each human being as they evolve to experience the innermost SELF. By putting on 'coats of skin', as the Bible states, Adam and Eve entered the lowest of the four worlds and became incarnate. This descent into matter was to be the first of four Journeys. The second is that of physical, psychological and spiritual development as they rise up towards the Divine Realm. One lifetime is clearly not enough to attain such an achievement. Therefore Kabbalah accepts the idea of reincarnation; that is, the soul being reborn into a new body after death and a period of reflection.

Called *Gilgulim* in Kabbalah, the process of transmigration over many generations enables individuals to learn more and help others on the Path to Self-realisation. This aiding is seen as the Third Journey. The final journey is that of the Resurrection when all humanity returns, at the End of Time, to the Absolute, having helped the Deity to perceive ITSELF in the complex mirror of Existence. This is possible because only humans can enter and exist simultaneously in all the worlds. Natural and supernatural beings, by their singular

Figure 13—FALL
Most presume that Adam and Eve were ejected from Paradise because they had
sinned. However, this was anticipated by the Creator who knew that the couple
would misuse their free will. The result was the first lesson about karma, called
"Measure for Measure" in Kabbalah. Besides, it may have been the only way to
get them out of the comfortable and pleasant environment of Paradise and down
to the Earthly world to begin their education. As Self-conscious agents of the
Absolute, they were to rise up through every level of Existence so as to aid God
to behold God in the Mirror of Existence. (Doré *Bible*, 19th century)

composition, are confined to their respective realities. What can an ape know of metaphysics or an angel understand about being in debt?

According to legend, in order to aid the return of Adam and Eve to the upper worlds the Archangel Raziel, whose title means 'The Secrets of God', was sent by God to give them a book that would tell them about the vast Ladder stretching between the highest and the lowest levels of Reality and how to use it. This knowledge was given by Enoch, alias Melchizedek, to Abraham and became the basis of monotheistic mysticism. Out of this arose many esoteric lines, each suitable not only for its place and time but every level of human evolution. Let those 'who have eyes to see and ears to hear' ponder the scriptures. The Bible is the most widely read of books because people sense there is something profound within its text. This is what Kabbalah is about. It contains Raziel's Book but one must learn how to discern the hidden lessons behind the stories that depict the best and worst of human nature.

Figure 14—TOWER OF BABEL
The Bible is full of symbols. Here humanity is in a phase of arrogance. When it developed to the level of a city state, it believed it could invade the upper Worlds. In psychological terms this is ego inflation, leading to delusion. This can occur in an individual or a whole culture. History is full of such events when people attain a new power and do not know its limit. Then confusion happens when connections are broken. This was the ancient period when organised warfare appeared and people who spoke a common Semitic tongue saw each other as competing enemies. Here is where Babel began. (Bank's Bible, 19th century.)

3. Lineage

Having arrived upon Earth, where Nature had evolved to a point when it could support a new form of organic life, early humanity had to learn how to live on the planet. Over millions of years they learnt to relate to the four elements of earth, water, air and fire and the basic laws of Nature. They then rose above the instinctive level of mere survival by planting crops and domesticating animals. No other creature prior to humans has exploited the environment in such a way. This event occurred because, unlike other creatures that were only aware of the present, mankind had the capacity to consider the past and ponder the future and, yet more important, become conscious of the invisible realms. Early man was aware of Nature spirits, the gods of the sky and even the possibility of an invisible other reality. This is clear from the objects left in graves and belief in an afterlife.

Primitive humanity world-wide subscribed, moreover, to a general view of Heaven and Hell, minor and major deities and even a Godhead. There was even an understanding of the law of consequences and good and evil. Stories in the Bible, like that of the murder of Abel by Cain and his punishment, indicate the emergence of a code of morality.

In the process of human evolution, be it individual or collective, correct conduct is crucial. Many Biblical stories illustrate that misconduct leads to destruction. This is epitomised by the episode of Sodom. But there is much more to this particular saga than the obvious. Lot's wife looks back, although she was told not to, and was turned into a pillar of salt. This is symbolically saying that if a person or society does not move on they can become crystallised and stuck in the past. This is fatal to any further development. Kabbalists have pondered the depths of many Biblical stories and discovered many layers of meaning, not only about the human condition but also its evolution, as in the case of Enoch and the non-Canonical legends about him. Many of these tales were recorded in the Talmud, that vast collection of writings concerned with legal matters, folklore and every

Figure 15—JACOB'S DREAM
Here a sleeping Jacob sees the celestial Ladder with 'angels' going up and down.
The word angel in Hebrew means a 'messenger' who can be either human or a
supernatural. The fact that these beings are ascending and descending is very
significant as it points out that there is a reciprocal flow between the upper and
lower Worlds, for example life, death and reincarnation which are part of
Kabbalistic doctrine. Of more immediate importance is the fact that Jacob is in
a psychic, not a mystic, state. This means he is as yet not spiritually awakened.
This comes when he is initiated by an 'angel' and is renamed Israel which signifies
a shift in level. The name can be translated as 'Champion of God'. (Bank's Bible,
19th century.)

Figure 16—BURNING BUSH
After learning how to look after sheep in the wilderness, a vital part of his training,
Moses is confronted by a miraculous phenomenon. This symbolises a contact
with the Divine as the bush is not consumed. Moreover, he is told that he is on
holy ground, another indication that his level of cognition has been raised. He is
told the reasons for his training in the Egyptian court in the art of leadership and
dealing with wild and tame animals in a difficult terrain. This is his destiny. For
this purpose he was saved from slaughter as an infant. Kabbalists would see this
as an indication of the moment of recognising their mission. (Bank's Bible, 19th
century.)

38

Figure 17—LEVELS
Here Moses and Aaron demonstrate before Pharaoh the difference between
magic and miracles. By swallowing the Egyptian priest's smaller snakes, they
illustrate how limited human capability is when compared to Divine power.
Pharaoh, in Kabbalah, represents the king of materiality that binds the soul,
represented by the Israelites who are his slaves. This is an analogue of the basic
human condition. No individual can develop until they realise that they are in
bondage. Then one can begin the journey to the Promised Land of enlightenment.
(Bank's Bible, 19th century)

facet of Jewish life over many centuries. Separate from this, as noted, was the oral line which transmitted the esoteric tradition. This was usually studied by those who wished to go deeper into the Torah.

Abraham was born in one of the world's first cities. Ur, in Mesopotamia, was a port, trading, manufacturing and cultural centre. He was, no doubt, educated there at one of the many schools where he learnt about the most advanced religious, philosophical and scientific ideas of the time. However, with the higher knowledge that had been imparted to him by Melchizedek, he added a totally new perspective which he passed on to Isaac, his son. Alas, Isaac became blind because he loved his earth-son Esau, who represented animal-level man, more than Jacob who had developed his soul. With the help of his wise mother, Rebekah, he took on the Teaching, symbolised by Isaac's Blessing for the First Born or fully human being.

Jacob recognised his mission when he saw, in a vision, the Great Ladder of Existence with various beings ascending and descending. He viewed it in a dream which meant that he was still spiritually asleep. This meant he was in a psychic state, not yet fully conscious of the transpersonal dimension of the cosmic and the Divine realms. His dream, however, is rich in esoteric information. The word 'Angel' in Hebrew means a 'messenger'. It does not clearly state whether such a being, in this context, is human or supernatural. Here also is a glimpse of the Four Journeys. These figures on the Ladder might be teachers or messengers coming down from the Higher Worlds or souls incarnating and discarnating in a Kabbalistic version of the Wheel of Life and Death. Such comings and goings have been in operation since Adam and Eve came down to Earth and will go on until the planet is no longer habitable.

Jacob's struggle with the Angel is another example that is full of meaning. Here the ordinary mind, the ego, can be seen wrestling with either his higher self or his discarnate teacher, known in Kabbalah as one's *maggid* or guardian angel. This episode was a crucial test about whether Jacob's inferior part could overcome his superior aspect. This is a struggle every Kabbalist has to contend with. After the event Jacob is renamed Israel which means to be, among other things, the 'Champion of God' or 'He who struggles with the Lord'. Jacob's family is a school of the soul with each of his twelve sons representing the entire range of human temperaments. When the Israelites go down to Egypt, the story takes on a new dimension. It becomes an allegory of becoming incarnate, that is when the soul becomes embodied. When

וינער ה' את מצרים בתוך הים. ובני ישראל הלכו ביבשה בתוך הים.

Figure 18—CROSSING THE RED SEA

This represents a crucial turning point in human development. There has to be a transitional moment of commitment to the Path of Self-realisation. The power of the physical Pharaoh's army has to be cut off. There is no turning back. Moses is, in this case, the Self who has to lead undisciplined and slave-minded sub-personalities across the purging desert of Sinai. Here most of those born and raised in Egypt will die off while a new and free generation will be born and become a unified nation or integrated psyche. (19th century Haggadah.)

Figure 19—MIRIAM'S SIN
Miriam, Moses' sister, possessed a psychic power, represented in Jewish folklore
by a movable well. She challenged her brother, claiming she was his equal. God
then called her, Aaron and Moses to appear in the Tabernacle. There, she was
smitten with leprosy for her conceit. This occurs when the ego believes it is on a
par with the Self. The result is that the lower mind is distorted by its sense of
importance and disaster ensues until it is cleansed of its presumption. (Bank's
Bible, 19th century.)

42

WEST.

NORTH.

SOVTHE.

EAST.

Figure 20—TABERNACLE

The design of this sacred structure given to Moses when on Mount Sinai is based upon the esoteric symbolism and metaphysical tradition that underlies Kabbalah. The Four Worlds are represented by the Holy of Holies or Emanation; the Sanctuary, Creation while the Courtyard symbolised the realm of Formation. Outside the precinct is the everyday world of Action. The priesthood was likewise divided according to the four levels of Existence. The High Priests represented the Divine; the priests, the Heavenly domain; the Levites, Paradise and the ordinary Israelite the physical dimension with each of twelve tribes standing for the twelve types of humanity. (Woodcut, 16th century.)

we are born, the soul is locked into the body. Over the early years our instincts and conditioning come to dominate our lives until the soul, represented by Moses, begins to remember that it came from the Holy Land of the Spirit. Legend has it that only the tribe of Levi recalled its ancient inheritance. Moses was a Levite but before he was shown his destiny he had to be trained in the ways of the world.

Moses was found by an Egyptian princess while other Israelite children were being massacred because it was foreseen by Egyptian priests that one of them would destroy the ruling caste and the army. Moses' adoption by the Pharaoh's sister was no accident but a providential event. This relates to a unique moment in some people's lives when they are presented with an opportunity that opens up an entirely new vista. It is often through a remarkable event that awakens them to what their life might be about. This is usually the culmination of some unconscious preparation, symbolised by Moses' education at Pharaoh's court. In his case it was to learn the art of leadership. In ordinary life it might be an accident or flash of enlightenment. For Moses it was when he saw an Israelite slave being tormented by an Egyptian taskmaster. By killing the Egyptian he was forced to leave the comfort of palace life and flee into the desert. Here he met Jethro who became his father-in-law and spiritual teacher. He taught Moses how to survive in the wilderness, the symbol of psychological desolation, without the accustomed support of a princely life. This corresponds to the state of a person who realises there is more to living than eating, begetting and all the games that go on between life and death.

According to legend, Jethro had a staff with ten jewels embedded in it which he had taken from the House of Joseph when in Egypt. This emblem of esoteric knowledge was given to Moses as a dowry when he married Jethro's daughter. Moses used this Holy Wand to demonstrate to Pharaoh that miraculous power was greater than the magic of the Egyptian priests. This was symbolised by Moses' great snake swallowing the magician's smaller serpents. It also reveals the difference between the psychic and spiritual realms, that is the personal and the transpersonal worlds of Formation and Creation.

The Book of Exodus is about the development of the psyche, as represented by the Israelites. The long time of forty years to cross the Sinai Desert, and the events of this journey, hint at the inner process of passing through the four levels within the mind. Each stage shows how a rabble and servile people undergo a profound transformation as

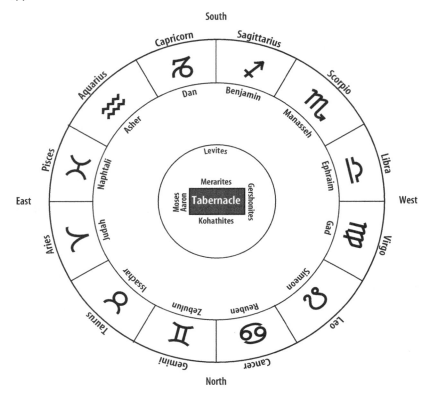

Figure 21—BIBLICAL ZODIAC
Astrology was part and parcel of ancient culture. While worship of the planetary gods was forbidden, astrology's principles were acknowledged as an early form of psychology. Thus each of Jacob's sons represented a particular temperament. The warlike Judah, for example, was Aries, Dan was assigned Capricorn and was to be a judge to the people. The Levites were not included in this scheme as they were to be the priestly clan that was meant to be above the influence of the stars. This view was later related to all Israel, meaning those who were not unconscious slaves of celestial influences. (Rabbinic text, 6th-7th century?)

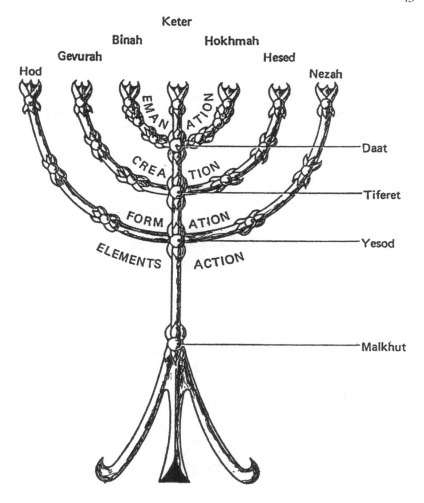

Figure 22—MENORAH
The design for a seven-branched candlestick to go into the Sanctuary of the Tabernacle—and later the Temple—is not just an object of great beauty. It contains the basic metaphysics of the Kabbalistic Tree of Life diagram. First, it is a solid gold unity, signifying the Divine realm. It has a right and left wing and a central pillar, indicating the three major principles that govern the balance of Existence. These, in turn, define the four worlds, while the twenty-two decorations represent the twenty-two paths that make up the triads. (Halevi.)

46

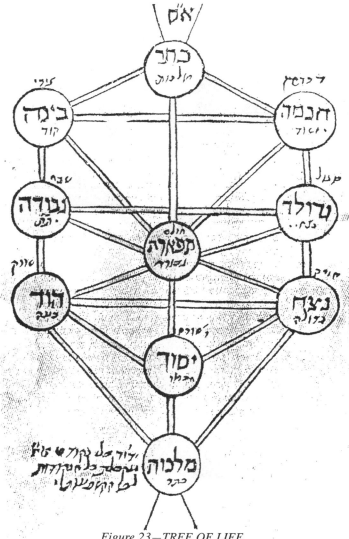

Figure 23—TREE OF LIFE

This is composed of the ten Sefirot or numbers indicated by the circles. They are
the key principles that work within the frame of Existence. Each of the twenty-
two letters of the Hebrew Aleph Bet are allocated to a path between the Sefirot,
also known as the Crowns, Hands of God, Holy Vessels and many other names.
The Tree is sometimes called the Garden of Holy Apples, the Face and Beard of
God and the Tree of Sapphires or Lights. There are various versions of the Tree
but this is the classical one in which every sefirah is part of a triad. (Cordovero,
16th century.)

a slave-minded generation die off before a free, strong nation can be born. During this period there are many back-slidings, rebellions and battles, as happens in psychological development. These relate to unco-ordinated sub-personalities within the psyche that want, out of habit, to cling to the old and familiar ways, even if it means continual suffering for those aspects of the mind that wish to grow. Take the remark of one disgruntled Israelite who said, 'At least in Egypt we did not go hungry'. Then there is the significant incident of Miriam, Moses' sister, symbol of the ego when she considers herself equal to the Soul, represented by her brother. She believed, because of her psychic abilities symbolised in Jewish folklore by a moveable well, that she, as the older, should be recognised as a power in her own right. Her lesson for her presumption was a hard one when she was afflicted by leprosy, a sign of corruption. In psychological terms this is a nervous breakdown when the ego is out of control during a crucial phase of spiritual evolution.

The ego governs the lower mind through conditioned habits and the compulsions of the instincts. This is seen as the vegetable level. With an increased degree of awareness a person rises to the animal level. This is seen in the battles fought with every rival, as represented by the Amalekites and other tribes. During this phase, discipline is vital for both physical and psychological survival. Finally comes the stage of becoming fully human, or an integrated nation, before leaving the tough training ground of the desert prior to entering the Spiritual Land flowing with milk and honey. Moses' forty days and nights spent on Mount Sinai, which represent Jacob's Ladder, transform him from a political leader into a great prophet. However, even he 'misses the mark' when he, at a crucial moment, forgets he is not the source of the 'Living Water' that sustains the Israelites. For this 'sin' he was not allowed, while incarnate, to cross the Jordan to enter the realm of the spirit.

Turning away from the symbolic approach we now touch upon the metaphysics of Kabbalah. Moses was given, on Mount Sinai, the Teaching that had almost been forgotten. The Tree of Life diagram dates from this event. It can be seen in the design of the golden seven-branched candlestick in the sanctuary, as specified by God. Its pattern, as seen in Figure 22, shows the two wings of the active and passive aspects of Existence and the central axis of equilibrium. There are seven candle holders and three central junctions of the arms, making ten in all. There is, however, if the base is regarded as a crucial

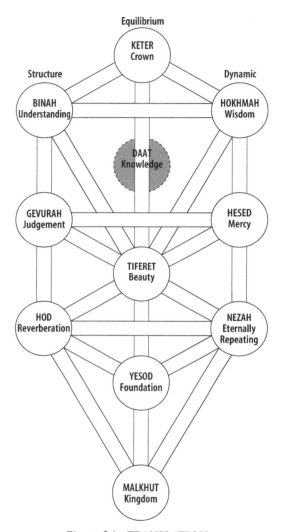

Figure 24—TRANSLATION

The Hebrew names are drawn from the Bible. However, their meaning is wide. The Crown, for example, is clearly the head and origin of all while the sefirot of Wisdom and Understanding represent an intellectual level of balance of Divine Law and Revelation. Just below comes what is called the non-sefirah of Knowledge or direct experience; while beneath it are the emotional sefirot, related to love and severity, or reward and punishment. At the centre is the co-ordinating pivot of Beauty. Below this, the translation of Hod and Nezah have the Hebrew root of 'to reverberate' and 'repeat'. The lowest two sefirot are likened to the foundation of a house and the ground it stands upon. (Halevi.)

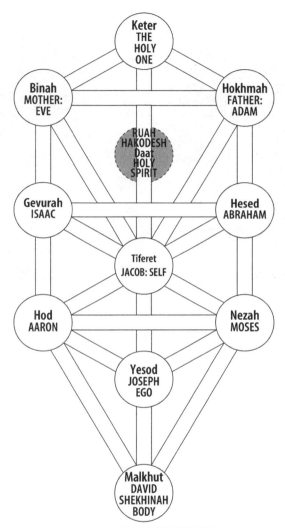

Figure 25—ARCHETYPES

In Kabbalah, certain Biblical characters are used as classic examples of human nature and the sefirot. The seven lower patriarchs, called the seven shepherds, represent the various types. Abraham loved God; Isaac feared God; while Jacob knew God. Moses and Aaron, in this scheme, are the two pillars of Israel while Joseph, the dreamer and Pharaoh's prime minister, represents the ego. King David is placed at the bottom as the man of blood and passion. At the top of the side pillars come Adam and Eve as the parents of humanity. In the highest central position is the Holy One while below it is the position of the Holy Spirit or Word of God. (Halevi.)

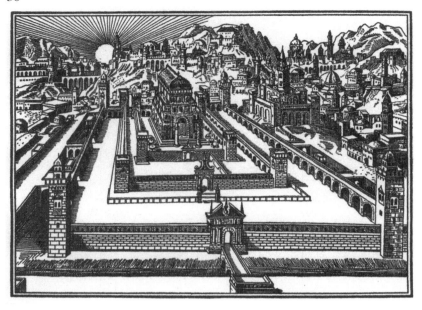

Figure 26—TEMPLE
In this idealised version of Solomon's Temple in Jerusalem, the four worlds are clearly defined. All are based upon a central long axis that runs through the outer and inner courts, the Sanctuary and the Holy of Holies. In the chambers set into the side walls, various non-ritualistic activities would take place, ranging from social occasions to study groups and mystical sessions. The priesthood were supreme here but there were the prophets and rabbis, not part of the priestly elite, who worked outside the religious establishment. (Jerusalem, 17th century)

element, an eleventh position just below the central crown. This was perceived by later Kabbalists as the place of Daat or direct mystical knowledge. The twenty-two decorations of the Menorah relate to the paths between the ten sefirot. Each path has a Hebrew letter assigned to it. Thus, it was said the universe was ordered according to the ten prime numbers and the twenty-two letters of the Aleph-Bet.

The ten Divine principles also lie behind the Ten Commandments. The bottom-most sefirah of Malkhut, the Kingdom, is about not coveting other's possessions while bearing false witness relates to the level of the ego at Yesod, as it is called. Hod and Nezah are concerned with not stealing or committing adultery; that is, taking without payment and not mixing things that should not be brought together. Tiferet, the sefirah at the centre of the Tree, is about murder. By this is meant that one should not maliciously seek to kill others, physically or psychologically, or destroy one's 'Self'. The commandment of Gevurah is about protecting and honouring one's parents or spiritual heritage while Hesed speaks of the Sabbath or making a sacred time and space. The three uppermost sefirot are concerned with the Godhead and how the Absolute should be regarded.

The Tabernacle itself was laid out according to the Four Kabbalistic Worlds. The outer court represented the realm of Nature; the Inner Court, the soul; while the sanctuary symbolised the World of the Spirit and the Holy of Holies, the Divine. Moreover, the four levels of the Israelite society of the common people, the Levites, priests and high priests symbolised, at least in theory, the levels of human development in regard to the physical, psychological, spiritual and Divine realms.

Solomon's Temple was also built according to the same plan with the two great columns of Mercy and Justice set on either side of the door of the Sanctuary. These represented the outer pillars of the Tree of Life while the long axis of the building was the middle pillar of Grace that ran through the centre of the two Courts, into the sanctuary and the dark, veiled chamber where the Ark was kept. During Solomon's time, Jerusalem was the spiritual capital of the world until he allowed one of his many wives, the Princess of Egypt, to place an idol within the Temple precinct. This act, to please a favourite spouse, undermined the Temple's integrity and exposed the exceptionally wise Solomon's fatal flaw by being seduced by excessive sensuality, symbolised by his huge harem. The result was a splitting up of his kingdom and the eventual destruction of the Temple.

The lesson here is that while a spiritual master may be great, even

52

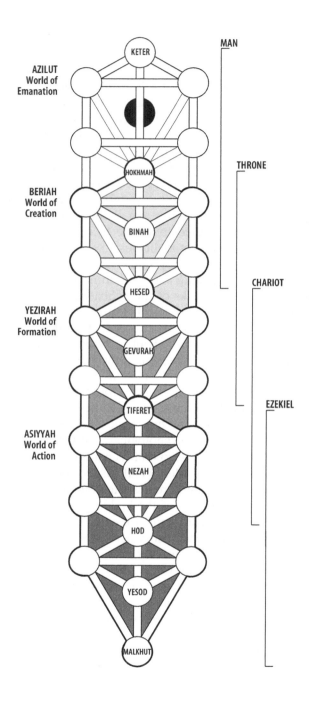

MAN

AZILUT
World of
Emanation

KETER

THRONE

BERIAH
World of
Creation

HOKHMAH

BINAH

CHARIOT

HESED

YEZIRAH
World of
Formation

GEVURAH

TIFERET

EZEKIEL

ASIYYAH
World of
Action

NEZAH

HOD

YESOD

MALKHUT

be one of the chain of Messiahs, it is possible to fall for what are known as the Lucific temptations of power, wealth and sex which cause others to suffer. Another example was King Saul, who disobeyed Samuel and died on his own sword, while even the next Anointed, David, lost the son he had by his adulterous relationship with Bethsheba. Because of other irresponsibilities, his son Absalom rebelled against him. The Bible is full of human follies. No one is above the law and beyond karma. Not a few great teachers have fallen by the wayside because of the temptation of inflation. The Bible is quite blunt about the realities of everyday life and the spiritual path. There is little or no sentimentality in the Old Testament. At times it seems to be excessively harsh but this is a warning about the consequences of karma. Moses, at the end of the five Books of Moses, sets out the situation and urges the Israelites to choose the Way of Life. The suffering that followed was not due to a severe God but humanity's stupidity and what it brought upon itself when it disregarded the Commandments.

Figure 27 (Left)—COSMIC SCHEME
Here the Divine Tree of Emanation is extended down in a specific sequence. In this the lower part of the superior world relates to the upper part of the realm immediately below. Thus there is a correspondence between them, even though they are quite separate realities. This means that a chain emerges from a Ladder that is held together by what is called the 'Kav' or Divine Line that is to be seen running down the centre column from the highest Crown. This fifth and Great Tree, as it is called, generates what are known as the Fifty Gates between the top and bottom of Existence. This is a metaphysical version of the symbolic Ezekiel's vision and Jacob's Dream. (Oral tradition)

Figure 28—CHARIOT RIDER
This depiction of Ezekiel's unique departure from Earth was seen as a model for Jewish mystics. The word Merkabah means chariot. This was the imaginary vehicle that consciousness would use to enter the invisible higher worlds. After fasting or some exercise to detach themselves from the body, the 'Chariot Rider', as they were called, would use the mind's eye to go down into the psyche in order to go up into the realm of the spirit. This required a great conscious effort but it was worth it, as they caught a glimpse or a full vision of Paradise and the seven Heavens, even Adam Kadmon. (Bank's Bible, 19th century.)

4. Early History

As a result of Solomon's error, his kingdom was divided and destroyed both by internal and external forces. The remnant of the people was exiled, ironically to distant Mesopotamia, the home of Abraham. This was a symbol of regression. Here they mourned the loss of Jerusalem and the Temple. However, the Teaching was not lost but manifested a new form in the vision of Ezekiel, a mystic of a priestly family. While sitting by the river Cheber he saw, emerging from the Heavens, the image of a vast chariot with wheels composed of eyes. This huge vehicle also had four iconic heads of a Man, Eagle, Lion and Bull at each corner. Above, myriads of angelic wings supported an enormous throne that filled the whole sky. Seated upon it, beneath a shimmering rainbow, was a tremendous humanoid figure made of fire which was accompanied by the sight and sound of flashing lightning and thunder.

The Biblical account of this awesome experience was studied later by Jews of the diaspora who were interested in its symbolism; for these clearly-defined four levels in the fiery Divine man, the Throne of Heaven, the Chariot and the Footstool of the Earth seemed to be related to the four Worlds depicted in the design of the Tabernacle and Temple. Some, more mystically inclined, went further and applied an ancient technique of imaginative contemplation used by Enoch. In this exercise, they went deep down into themselves in order to 'Ride the inner Chariot', as it was called, up into the Higher worlds. These spiritual excursions told them much about the order and inhabitants of Hell, Paradise and the Heavens. Descriptions of the various ranks and functions of the angels and demons were recorded, as were the conditions of humans who had died or were yet to be reborn. These observations were written down in what become known as the *Hekalot* books of the Heavenly Halls.

It was during this period of exile, about the fifth century Before the Common Era (BCE), that a new Hebrew alphabet came into use. This, it is said, was specially designed to relate to the twenty-two paths of the Tree of Life. Each letter, like every sacred number of the sefirot,

Figure 29—ADAM KADMON

This vast radiant figure was sometimes described in mathematical measurements. The idea was that the numbers and proportions would give some notion of Laws of the Divine realm. Many rabbis argued about the veracity of this obscure text because they took it literally. They had never had a mystical encounter with the Divine. This was a problem for those who had, for how could they describe the indescribable? Mystics of other traditions had the same difficulty when they presented their experience in terms of their culture. For example, the Chinese circular symbol containing Yan and Ying is an attempt to define the three principles that govern Existence. Here an image of words has been shaped to convey an awesome impression of Adam Kadmon. (Hebrew Text, medieval.)

Final Letters.	Figure.	Names.	Corresponding Letters.	Numerical Power.
Mother	א 1	Aleph	- - -	1
Double	ב } 2	Baith	B	2
	ב	Vaith	V	- -
	ג 3	Gimmel	G	3
	ד 4	Daleth	D	4
	ה 5	Hay	H	5
	ו 6	Wav	W	6
Single	ז 7	Zayin	Z	7
	ח 8	Cheth	Ch	8
	ט 9	Teth	T	9
	י 10	Yood	Y	10
Double	כ } 11	Caph	C	20
		Chaph	Ch	- -
Single	ל 12	Lamed	L	30
Mother	מ 13	Mem	M	40
	נ 14	Noon	N	50
Single	ס 15	Samech	S	60
	ע 16	Ayin	- - -	70
Double	פ } 17	Pay	P	80
		Phay	Ph	- -
Single	צ 18	Tzadè	Tz	90
	ק 19	Koof	K	100
Double	ר 20	Raish	R	200
Mother	ש } 21	Sheen	Sh	300
		Seen	S	- -
Double	ת } 22	Tav	T	400
		Thav	Th	- -

Figure 30—LETTERS AND NUMBERS

In the ancient world, certain letters corresponded to particular numbers. Due to classical Greek influence which the Jews could not avoid, various systems of Biblical interpretation, according to letter-number matchings, were adopted. These sought to find the hidden secrets of the words of the Torah. However, these methods of, for example, Gematria and Notaricon could lead into blind intellectual alleys. The fact that the numerical value of Metatron, 314, equalled that of the Divine Name SHADDAI was not a convincing proof, as many other words could add up to the same number. Unfortunately, this approach was seen later as a traditional part of Kabbalah when in fact it originated in Alexandria. (Correspondences, 19th century.)

58

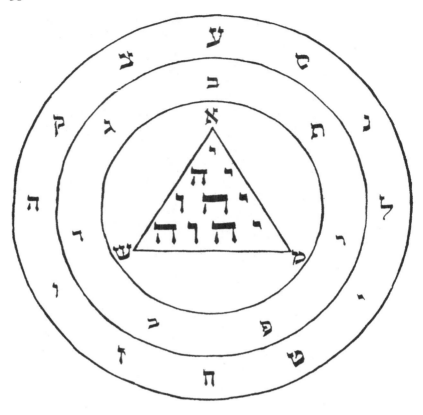

Figure 31—ADOPTION
It was not uncommon in the ancient and medieval world for cultures to borrow
or even steal from each other. The notion, for example, of the Resurrection is
Persian, as is that of the Messiah. Here in this diagram is a mixture of Hebrew
letters, astrology and Pythagoras. The outer circle letters define the Zodiac
whereas the second circle has a letter for each of the then known celestial bodies.
The innermost circle contains the Kabbalistic equivalent of the Chinese and
Hindu concepts of the three principles that control Creation. Here they are set
out in the Hebrew letters Aleph, Shin and Mem. They relate to the triangle, inside
which is a Pythagorean arrangement of the Holy Name, YHVH. This defines the
increasing complexity of the four worlds, headed by the letter Yod or number ten.
(Book of Formation, 6th–7th century/Prof. James Russell)

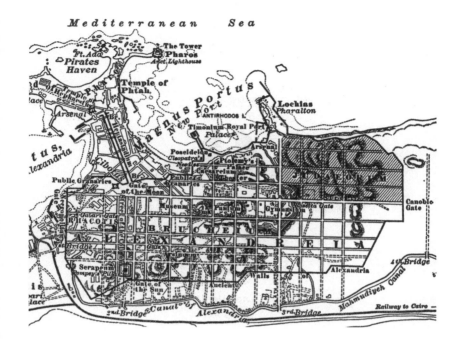

Figure 32—ALEXANDRIA
This port, industrial and cultural city was home to many cultures. Here were to
be found influences from as far away as Persia, India and China. Forty per cent
of the population was Jewish. The museum or university held public lectures on
Saturday afternoons because many Jews came. The city was, at one time, the
spiritual capital of the world and had several important schools of the soul
within its walls which exchanged concepts and practices. One inhabitant, Philo,
a master Jewish scholar educated in the Greek manner, reviewed the Bible from
an Hellenic angle that was greatly to influence the Church and later Kabbalah.
(Jewish Encyclopaedia 20th century.)

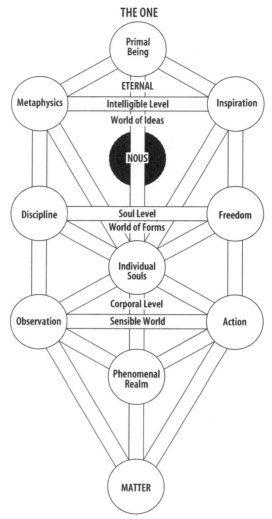

Figure 33—HELLENISM
When Alexander the Great conquered Egypt, the Levant and Western Asia, Greek culture took over as a dominant culture. The Hellenic intellectual approach of philosophy attracted some of the Jewish intelligentsia, as it was the perfect counter balance to the mythological and legal approach of the orthodox Jewish establishment. The rational approach was set out here on the Tree, according to the sefirotic qualities. At the head is the Divine ONE. On the right is the more inspirational Platonic approach; on the left the more analytical Aristotelian viewpoint. Down the centre is the amalgam of both and the more mystical Neo-Platonic mode of perception. (Halevi.)

had a particular meaning according to the pen stroke that composed it. Also introduced during this time was the idea of the Messiah and the notion of a Day of Judgement and the Resurrection. These concepts came from the Zoroastrian mystical tradition. Such adaptations and exchanges with other esoteric lines were not uncommon in the Biblical period. Solomon's Temple had been built by Phoenicians while Gematria and other letter-number systems of interpretation adopted later were borrowed from the Hellenic culture. The terms and methodology are Greek and probably originated in Alexandria. In the ancient world, everyone borrowed what was useful and made it their own. A classic example in Jewish mysticism is the *Sefer Yetzirah* or *Book of Formation*.

This slim volume, although traditionally accredited to Abraham, is full of Babylonian and Greek symbols. In its concentrated text, the book sets out a picture of the universe and the microcosm of a human being. The body, for example, was related to the four elements and the Solar system with the Sun, Moon, planets and zodiacal signs seen as reciprocal parts of an organic and cosmic process. Again, contrary to modern orthodox Jewish belief, astrology was a study that was an accepted part of ancient and medieval rabbinic culture. The rabbinic commentaries of the Talmud openly refer to it but never in a systematic way although, in popular Jewish idiom, the expression *Mazzel Tov* or 'Congratulations' actually means the 'good stars' or planets have benefited one.

Another mystical concept to emerge in the early centuries of the Common Era (CE) was the notion that the size of the humanoid figure of Ezekiel's vision, according to a book called the *Shiur Komah*, could be calculated. However, some rabbis took the scheme of measurements literally instead of metaphorically. This led to a great debate without any conclusion. Without a background of the esoteric Teaching or the metaphysics of the Tree and Jacob's Ladder, the proportions of what was called the *Kavod* or Glory of God made no sense. Even the great scholar, Saadia Gaon, declared this fiery figure was a mystery to him. So too was the notion of reincarnation which was a nonsense to his brilliant but literal mind.

In Alexandria, around the time of the second Temple, a Jewish writer, Philo, applied the Greek philosophical approach and method to the Old Testament. He recognised the Bible as being a Divine allegory in which, for example, the patriarchs were living symbols of certain principles. It was because of his influence that the NAME or WORD

Figure 34—PLOTINUS
Born in Alexandria in the 3rd century of the Common Era he, it is said, was half
Greek and half Jew. It is believed by some that he was a reincarnation of Plato,
returned to complete his mission. He brought together the opposing perceptions
of revelation and reason into a mystical and metaphysical form that set out very
clearly the doctrine of the Chain of Being. This was adapted by later Kabbalists
in defining more precisely the composition of Jacob's Ladder. His recorded talks
about his own mystical experience give his work an authority not found in most
religious or philosophical texts of the period. It is he who said there was no
religion higher than Truth. (Roman portrait bust.)

Figure 35—DESTRUCTION
When the Romans destroyed the second Temple, the aristocracy of the priesthood
lost their mandate of authority. The rabbis of often more humble origin then took
over. However, the esoteric tradition, drawn from both classes, continued
discreetly, not only in Judea but throughout the now widely scattered Jewish
Diaspora. The main focus of these schools shifted to Mesopotamia where the
Merkabah line flourished behind the façade of the scholarly academies. Here the
theory and practices were adapted to new conditions, absorbing what could be
learnt from Islam which now became the dominant culture in the area. (Arch of
Titus, 1st century.)

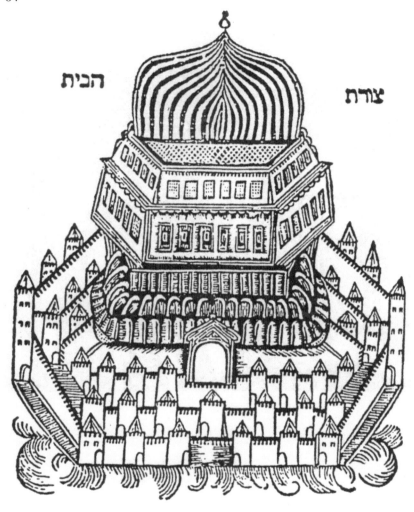

הבית **צורת**

Figure 36—DOME OF THE ROCK

When Islam conquered the Holy Land it built a huge mosque on the ruined Temple site. Much of Mohammed's religion was based upon Jewish and Christian mythology, legend and customs. His Night Ascent from the Temple Mount was exactly parallel to that of the Chariot Riders. The descriptions of Paradise, the Halls and Heavens and their angelic and human inhabitants were also adopted. However, as with Kabbalah, certain esoteric Greek and Persian ideas were incorporated and gave rise to Sufism, the mystical line of Islam. This image, which appears on the front of and in some old Jewish books, is not the Temple but the Mosque of Omar on Temple Mount. (Jewish woodcut, 16th century.)

Figure 37—CELESTIAL LETTERS
It was believed by some Jews that the stellar configurations were ancient Hebrew words. The problem was how to read them. This idea was rooted in the first Jewish treatise on cosmology, the Sefer Yetzirah *or* Book of Formation. *In this slim volume the letters, zodiac, celestial bodies and aspects of the body were seen as the key to understanding a complex cosmic system. However, without the background of Kabbalah, the book became a religious relic. Every esoteric tradition has this folk level which is usually a garbled and superstitious version of profound universal principles.* (Woodcut, 17th century.)

Figure 38—ASTROLOGY
This subject is as old as Kabbalah. Ur, the city where Abraham came from, was renowned for its university's reputation in astronomy and astrology. When Islam became the dominant culture of the Middle East, it combined Greek science and philosophy with the ancient study of the heavens into its theology. As most of the Jews lived within the Islamic domain, they became involved in all the new developments due to this synthesis of traditions. Indeed, some rabbis became leading experts in calculating celestial movements and their influence on human affairs. While regarded as superstition by the scholarly elite, they were never accused of worshipping the stars. After all, Abram had been a master astrologer. (Woodcut, 16th century.)

of GOD, when translated into Greek, was called the LOGOS. This was picked up by the early Christian Fathers who made it a key part of Church doctrine. Ironically, the rabbinic community more or less ignored his work until the Middle Ages when it was to have a considerable impact on Kabbalah.

Another important Alexandrian was Plotinus who, it is said, was half-Greek and half-Jewish. He studied under a master called Amonaius Saccus whose names are a Greek version of the Egyptian god, Amun, and Isaacs. He, too, was probably of mixed blood; not unusual in a city where 40 per cent of the population was Jewish and people mingled from all over the known world. Out of this cosmopolitan melting pot of religion, philosophy and mysticism came Neo-Platonism with its idea of Existence emanating from the Godhead to produce a vast chain of Worlds and beings. It is believed by some scholars that Neo-Platonism was an amalgam of Hellenic, Egyptian, Jewish and possibly Hindu mysticism and metaphysics, as well as Persian and Buddhist concepts and practices. All these elements were present in ancient Alexandria which was famous for its museum, library and high culture.

When Islam conquered Western Asia and North Africa, Baghdad became not only the political capital of a new kind of civilisation but, like Alexandria, a spiritual centre. Here the Moslem intelligentsia studied Persian, Christian and Jewish religious ideas and methods, as well as Greek science and philosophy. The Hellenic view of knowledge, in particular, had such an appeal to the Arab mind that one of the Caliphs collected all the texts his agents could find and had them translated into Arabic. As Arabic had become the *lingua franca* of the Middle East, Jews also began to read the classical Greek texts. They, like the Moslems, were impressed by the precision of Plato, Aristotle and other Greek thinkers and adopted with relish the Hellenic Way of Reason. However, as with the Moslem intelligentsia, they were confronted by a crucial question. Which was the final authority as regards Truth? Their respective scriptures of revelation claimed to be the ultimate authority but one could not ignore the rational conclusions of observation and logic. Religious fundamentalists held the view, for example, that the ground was wet because God willed it. It was considered heresy by some to suggest it was because of rain. Fierce debates in both communities split them into opposing camps.

The Jewish philosopher Maimonides tried to reconcile religion and philosophy in a book called the *Guide to the Perplexed*. However, his

Figure 39—ABRAHAM IBN EZRA
Born in Spain, he was a rabbi, scholar, poet, philosopher and astrologer. He
wandered with his astrolabe, an instrument for ascertaining the positions of the
heavenly bodies, all over the Middle East and Western Europe. Besides being the
first to analyse the Bible in a new way, he wrote a text on astrology from which
this illustration is taken. He introduced a Jewish version of Neo-Platonism to
every rabbinic school he visited. This, like the work of Solomon ibn Gabirol, an
earlier Jewish Neo-Platonic poet and scholar, was to have a profound influence
on what was to become Kabbalah. Unlike the old mythological Merkabah line, it
has an intelligible order and precision. (Medieval manuscript.)

careful, intellectual approach outraged many devout Jews as he indicated that only the intelligentsia would enter the higher Heavens. Such was the passion aroused by this, now quite serious, battle between faith and philosophy that his books were burnt as they influenced the young to turn away from religion and seek the more attractive pursuit of Greek philosophy and science. This phenomenon led many into a more secular way of life and even conversion.

Meanwhile, the Jewish-Andalusian poet and philosopher, Ibn Gabirol, who wrote a book on Neo-Platonic themes, composed a long liturgical poem, *Keter Malkhut* (*The Crown and Kingdom*) setting out Jacob's Ladder of the various Worlds in astrological and metaphysical terms. It was he who solved the philosophical problem of how the Absolute related to the relative Worlds by introducing the notion of Divine Will which acted as the intermediary between Existence and the NO-THING-NESS of the Godhead.

His views, and those of other Jewish and Arabic philosophers, were taken from Southern Spain by a family of Jewish translators who were fleeing from Moslem fundamentalists to South Western France. Here they translated various texts for the Jewish mystical circles that resided there. These schools had been working with the mystical line brought in from Germany that had come, originally via Italy, from the Middle East. This tradition was based upon the old Merkabah or Ezekiel Chariot approach. This had been carried from Italy over the Alps by the rabbinic Kalonymos family who had received the Teaching from Aaron of Baghdad, a wandering mystic, in the ninth century. The Kalonymos had finally settled in Germany where they founded a school of the soul on the Rhine. Here the Merkabah line took root in a prosperous Jewish community that had been there since Roman times. However, during the Crusades it was devastated by mobs who saw the Jews as infidels and, egged on by the Church, the killers of Christ. The then-head of the clan had the essentials of the oral Teaching written down so that it would not be lost. This was taken by some Jews who escaped massacre to the South-West of France where there was an unusually high degree of tolerance at the time of the Cathars, a breakaway Christian sect with a mystical base.

It was in this area that the Jewish mythical line of the Merkabah met the philosophical stream coming up from Spain. Here, it is said, a certain Jacob HaNazir of Lunel received a visit from Elijah who initiated him into the secrets of Existence. This may well have happened in a moment of illumination but it must also be taken into

Figure 40—TOLEDO
This city in central Spain was, for a period during the early Middle Ages, the spiritual capital of the West. Here the Moslems, Jews and Christians met in a cultural equality. At the royal court, in the university and private homes, discussions about philosophy, religion, science and art went on between the three traditions. As a result, translations of Hellenic thought, medicine and alchemy were produced. In a room above a tavern, a Jew might take the words of an Arabic reader and turn them into Castilian for a Christian scholar who would write them down in Latin. Just as significant, ancient and new esoteric ideas were discussed and adapted by the mystics of each religion for their particular line. (Bridge and fortress, 19th century print.)

Figure 41—SYNAGOGUE
This Toledan Place of Assembly not only had religious and social gatherings
within it but it was also where any Jew from abroad could come and meet his
co-religionists and be welcome and contact fellow mystics as well. Toledo had a
reputation for this preoccupation, in the same way that Montpellier in France
was famed for its school of medicine and Bologna was known for its reputation
in legal studies. As can be seen by the style of architecture, Islamic influence is
strong. Indeed, the Moslems and Jews of this period got on particularly well and
shared at this point their Hellenic knowledge freely with Christians. It was a
Golden Epoch. (Maria Blanca, 13th century.)

72

Figure 42—DEBATE
Discussions between Christians and Jews could take two forms. The negative was when churchmen tried to persuade Jews that Jesus was the Messiah. The positive exchanges between scholars were usually more discreet. For example, it is known that the physician to one medieval King of England had private conversations with an abbot about philosophy. Another was that the Jewish rabbis of Chartres talked with the monks and builders of the cathedral which appears to have influenced the design of the building. In this figure, the Jews are distinguished by their pointed hats which they were obliged to wear to mark them out. Despite this segregation, individuals interested in the Truth, it seems, got together. (Medieval woodcut.)

Figure 43—GERONA
In this North-Eastern Spanish city there was a remarkable rabbinic school. Many of its scholars had had contact with the local university which is just a few streets away. This meant that they were well acquainted with the philosophical approach to religion that arose in the Golden Islamic period. When the controversy over which was superior, Revelation or Reason, then going on within Jewry as well as Islam and Christendom, reached a crisis point the rabbis of Gerona, a certain Azriel ben Menaham in particular, published a Neo-Platonic version of the Teaching to bring about a reconciliation. It was from this time, the 12th century, that the name Kabbalah was used. (Synagogue Street, 13th century)

Figure 44—ZOHAR

This set of books was an encyclopaedia of Kabbalah. It was composed of many strands and fragments of the Jewish esoteric tradition and synthesised by its editor, Moses de Leon. It drew upon ancient texts and new philosophical formulations. It was cast in the form of a rabbinic commentary within the frame of a series of discussions that take place in various locations in the Holy Land. While some saw it as a genuine document of the Roman period, others regarded it as a brilliant fake, due to its artificial language and references to events and people that had not yet occurred. Even so, it was revered as it contained the Teaching. (Printed edition, 16th century.)

account that the devout Jacob, on a pilgrimage to Jerusalem, had encountered a Jewish international community of rabbis who were particularly interested in Neo-Platonism. When he came back to France he transmitted what he had learnt to a small group that began to integrate the mythical and philosophical streams of the Teaching into a unified whole.

One of the leading lights of the area was Isaac the Blind who coined many new terms for what was to become known as Kabbalah. It was he who invented the definition AYN SOF for the Absolute. Among his students was a Spanish Jew, Azriel of Gerona who, upon his return home, produced a carefully ordered form of what he had learnt. This he cast in the Hellenic mode, like Ibn Gabirol, of question and answer about the origin and nature of Existence. Some of his writings he published while he lectured during his travels around Spain about the new formulation. Isaac objected to such material being brought into the public domain where, he said, it would be inevitably distorted but it was too late. The study of Kabbalah had caught the imagination of the Jewish intelligentsia as well as the mystic groups to be found throughout the Iberian Peninsula.

The reason for this was that the Spanish Jews were, on the whole, more educated than the French or German Jews because every major city in Spain had a university. The one in Gerona, for example, was just around the corner from the synagogue. Azriel hoped that by presenting the esoteric Teaching in an academic way he would check the trend of the educated from drifting away from their Jewish roots. The blend of Reason and Revelation offered by Kabbalah indeed met a deep need and it suddenly blossomed into a great religious movement.

From here on, Kabbalah in Spain spread far and wide. Its novel mode of philosophical symbolism had such appeal that many rabbis began writing up their version of what was claimed to be an ancient tradition. Because of this phenomenon, an esoteric group in the city of Guadalajara decided to produce an encyclopaedic work that would bring various views together into a unified picture. Moses de Leon was probably commissioned to be the editor. He took both traditional and contemporary material and fused it into the many volumes of *The Zohar* which soon became a best seller because it claimed to be the work of a Rabbi Ben Yohai who had lived in Roman-occupied Palestine.

This did not fool some scholars who noted that both Christian and Moslem elements were indirectly mentioned and even quoted. Also,

76

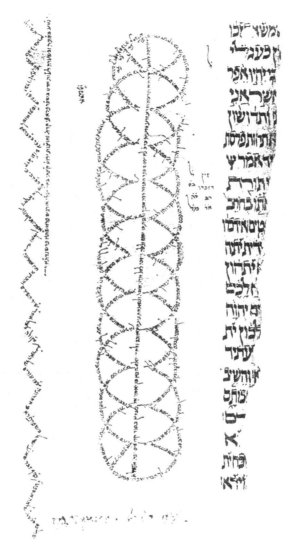

Figure 45—COMMUNICATION
This Jacob's Ladder made up of Biblical texts is a page from a document from the Yemen. This port at the tip of Southern Arabia was a trading post between the Occident and Orient and part of a vast Jewish commercial network. Not only did goods and services pass along the land-sea routes but also letters and books. This example is clearly Neo-Platonic and Kabbalistic with its eleven interpenetrating circles that take into account the non-sefirah of Daat (Knowledge) and the central axis of the Divine Kav line. (Yemeni manuscript, 15th century.)

descriptions of certain places in the Holy Land were closer to Spain than Palestine. Indeed, one man came all the way from the Middle East to verify the original manuscript Moses de Leon claimed he possessed. Indeed, he declared that his life should be forfeit if he lied. When Isaac of Acre arrived in Avila, he found that Moses had died. His widow said that *The Zohar* had all come out of her husband's head and that he had used the name of such an eminent, ancient rabbi to give *The Zohar* a certain authenticity. This was not an uncommon practice of the period. *The Zohar* became even more well-known when the Jews were expelled from Spain in 1492 and the work was printed in Italy. Parts were then translated into Latin. Kabbalah could now be studied by the Christians who were convinced that this forgotten Jewish mystical tradition could revive the Catholic Church's flagging spiritual reputation in the face of a growing Protestant revolt.

78

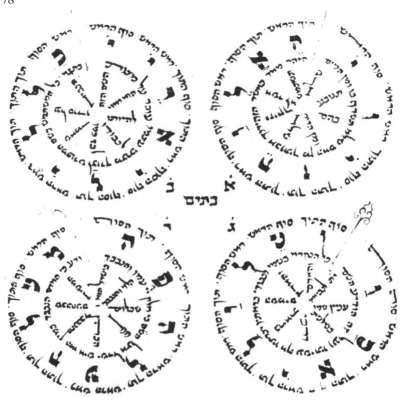

Figure 46—ABULAFIA

He was a Jewish mystic who wandered all around the Mediterranean. However, as a Kabbalist he was not so interested in the metaphysics of the Tree as the practical use of the Hebrew letters. These were used either in a mandala form, as illustrated here, or to be turned over and over in the mind during meditation until consciousness reached a point of stillness in the Self amid the activity of a fully occupied ego. Unfortunately, without the structure of the Tree, this mode of practice can become disorienting. Indeed, it is recorded that he tried to convert the Pope and only escaped execution when the pontiff suddenly died. Abulafia was seen as insane and was released from prison. (Manuscript, 13th century.)

5. *Later History*

When a young Italian aristocrat, Pico della Mirandola, was fascinated by what he heard about Kabbalah, he hired a Jewish scholar to translate parts of *The Zohar* and other Kabbalistic texts. He then proceeded to reorient the system, symbolism and metaphysics so that Jesus became the centre. This gave rise to what became known as Christian Cabala. Mirandola hoped this would convince the Church that he had rediscovered the esoteric secrets that it had lost. Unfortunately, with popes like Alexander VI, a Borgia who held orgies in the Vatican, such spiritual mysteries made little impression. Had he and other popes taken on the Teaching, it might have offset the Reformation.

There was, however, another line born out of the discovery of Kabbalah by Europeans. This was due to a German scholar, Reuchlin, who wrote in detail about the Tradition and how it could be applied to salvation. This was taken up by the Protestant and Catholic intelligentsia who incorporated parts and methods of Kabbalah into a new theology. Out of this arose a number of different schools of the soul that gave rise to the Rosicrucians, Martinists and individuals like Jacob Boehme, whose mysticism was clearly influenced by Kabbalah.

Yet another non-Jewish line of Kabbalah was to emerge. This was set out by Agrippa, an eclectic scholar who was interested in the practical aspect of Kabbalah in applying its principles to the occult. His work was to become the basis of the Western magical tradition. Another manifestation of Kabbalah's influence was the card pack called the Tarot. In Hebrew this means 'Teachings'. This graphic system had four suits that represented the four worlds. Each of these was made up of ten cards with four court cards to symbolise the four levels present in every world. This set was called the minor Arcana. Then there were the major Arcana, made up of twenty-two picture cards. To each of these was designated a Hebrew letter and an archetypal image such as Death, Initiation, the Stars and many occult symbols. They were a mixture of Hermetic, magical and Kabbalistic themes that defined cosmic forces, phases of development and esoteric events.

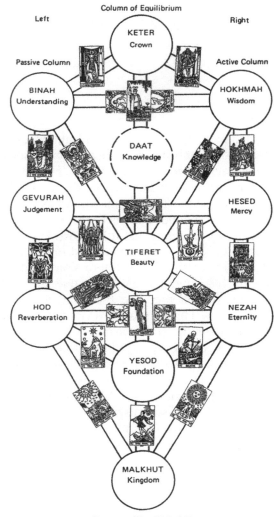

Figure 47—TAROT

Once Kabbalah came into the public domain it was used and misused in many ways. The word 'tarot' in Hebrew means 'teachings'. This pack of cards was based upon Kabbalah and Hermetism. It was created by some occult school of the soul in this form to avoid the Inquisition. It is composed of the Minor Arcana of four suits of ten cards, representing the four Worlds with four cards in each symbolising the levels within. The pictorial Major Arcana uses the Hebrew letters that relate to the paths and archetypal images to illustrate universal principles. Later it was seen as a game and used as an oracle by those who sensed its hidden dimension. (Tarot on the Tree, source unknown.)

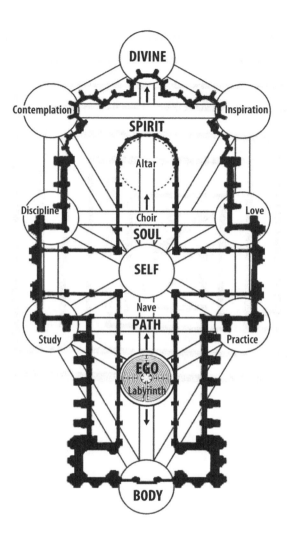

Figure 48—GROUND PLAN
The cathedral of Chartres was not only one of the first medieval gothic buildings,
it was a school of the soul. The pattern of its ground plan is so close to that of
the Tree that it cannot be just a coincidence. This connection is possible because
the Jewish quarter was just across the street and had several eminent scholars in
residence while it was being built. There must have been some collusion between
the monks and rabbis during a period of mutual respect. The famous labyrinth is
an archetypal symbol for the wandering lower mind of the ego while the triad of
the choir represents the soul and the altar the place of mystical experience.
(Discovered by Prof. Keith Critchlow.)

Figure 49—CORDOVERO
After the expulsion of Jews from Spain in 1492, many Kabbalists migrated to the Galilean town of Safed in the Holy Land where they set up schools of the soul. Moses Cordovero was a leading member and writer in the 16th century who produced a major work called The Garden of Pomegranates. *This contained all the Kabbalistic material known up to that point, as well as his own contribution. This figure is one of his illustrations. It is the Tree of Life made up of the first Hebrew letter of each sefirah; Keter the Crown enclosing, in a series of shells, all the other letters, down to Malkhut, the Kingdom at the centre. This echoed the concept of each world being like a kernel within a nut and so on, in a descending chain.* (Cordovero, 16th century.)

The Tarot appeared to have been created by a school that wished to avoid the attention of the Inquisition by concealing them as a card game.

In the 16th century, Jewish exiles from Spain congregated in the Galilean hill town of Safed which had become the Kabbalistic capital for the Diaspora. One school was founded by an eminent lawyer, Joseph Caro, who had the psychic capacity to act as the mouthpiece of a discarnate teacher. This is a Kabbalistic technique that only the well-trained and mature should practice. In contrast was Moses Cordovero, a master scholar and mystic who gathered all he could find in Kabbalah into a dense metaphysical book called *The Garden of Pomegranates*. This he completed before he was thirty. Clearly he was an old soul, remembering what he had learnt in previous lives. It is generally believed one should not study Kabbalah until one is forty.

Into this circle of Kabbalists came Isaac Luria who had been brought up in Egypt. He had spent a great deal of time alone on an island in the Nile, contemplating *The Zohar*. During such periods of isolation he had several revelations. One made him believe he was the current Messiah who had come to introduce a new kind of Kabbalah. When Cordovero, his teacher, died, Luria set up his own group and began to teach a doctrine that stated that the Divine Sefirotic Tree had been shattered when the power of the first emanations had broken the seven lower vessels. This, Luria claimed, had caused the organisation of Existence to be distorted as sparks of Divinity fell and were scattered throughout the lower Worlds. This, he maintained, explained the origin of Evil and cruelty in history. The idea had great appeal to Jews who had suffered devastating persecution for centuries. So it was that Lurianic Kabbalah came to overshadow the classical integrated tradition symbolised by Jacob's Ladder. It became very popular, moreover, because Luria offered salvation, in that Jews could help in the reconstruction of Existence by pious deeds and certain new practices. Here it is interesting to note that Luria died of the plague before he reached forty. However, many fantastic legends about him enhanced his reputation after his death. Over time he became the model for a charismatic master rabbi. This occurs when people seek a saviour in dire times.

The elegant and simple system of Jacob's Ladder was almost forgotten while various versions of Luria's scheme were seen as the authentic Kabbalistic tradition. Many learned rabbis were convinced by Luria's explanation about the disruption of Existence, ignoring the

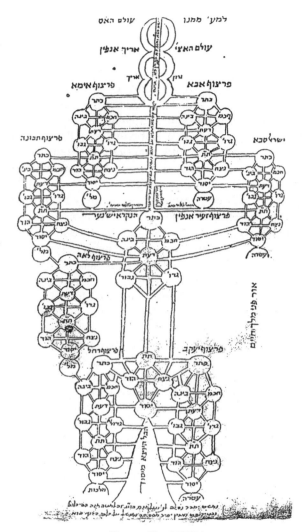

Figure 50—LURIA

He was a student of Cordovero's but he had his own ideas. Breaking with the tradition of Existence being a unity, he said that the origin of evil was that when the Divine influx filled the vessels of the Sefirot, they shattered the unity of Existence. This figure is based upon Luria's view, even though the Torah states quite clearly that God 'saw that Creation was good...very good'. Here began a split in the tradition as many people believed the shattering was the cause of so much suffering. Luria's view became accepted as the authentic version, even though it only dated back to the 16th century and a man who believed he was the Messiah. (Manuscript, 16th century.)

Figure 51—CHRISTIAN KABBALAH
During the Italian Renaissance a certain nobleman, Pico della Mirandola, a scholar,
upon discovering Kabbalah believed it held the esoteric key the Church had lost.
Mirandola and two German scholars, Reuchlin and Agrippa, spread the word
about Kabbalah throughout Western Christendom, about to fight a cruel war
over doctrine. For a time, Kabbalah was in fashion among the intelligentsia.
Here Christ is at the centre of a circular Tree with the Pythagorean triad of the
Name of God at the top. Despite the Hebrew to give it an authenticity, it is a
Christian version of the Tradition. (Heinrich Khunrath, 16th century.)

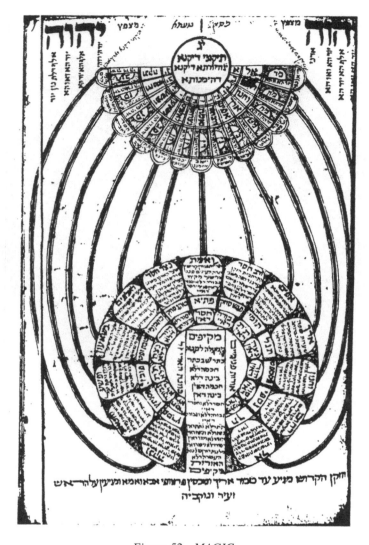

Figure 52—MAGIC
Every esoteric tradition has its level of superstition. Kabbalah is no exception.
Here the thirteen Attributes of God, in a Kabbalistic format, are used in an image
to keep away evil. Kabbalah was used by European occultists to bring heathen
and pagan folk beliefs and practices within an overall scheme. From this arose
a variety of magical lines that mixed alchemy, astrology and sorcery. From this
arose high and low occultism. These ranged from the making of protective
amulets to elaborate rituals within secret ceremonies that sought to make contact
with the invisible powers. (Jewish amulet, 17th century.)

Torah and the words in Genesis that God had said; that Creation was *Tov Meod*—very good.

Because of the terrible war between Catholic and Protestant, in which Christian murdered Christian, and a huge massacre of Jews in Eastern Europe it was believed by many that the End of the World was imminent. Before this occurred, Jewish tradition said, the last Messiah would appear to take them home to the Holy Land. There had been at least ten false messiahs down the centuries but they had all failed to deliver. However, in the 17th century there appeared in the Turkish empire a charismatic young man who claimed he was the expected Anointed. His name was Shabbetai Zvi.

At this point a so-called Kabbalist from Gaza, called Nathan, saw the opportunity to be a John the Baptist to Shabbetai Zvi and backed his cause using the Lurianic ideas. Within a short time and despite rabbinic opposition, Shabbetai Zvi's campaign generated a powerful attraction. Jews as far away as Holland made ready to sell up and follow him to Jerusalem. However, when the Sultan's secret police realised this Messianic figure could be a threat to the Turkish state, as other minorities might follow the Jews' example, they arrested Shabbetai Zvi. He was given the choice to become a Moslem or to die. When he instantly converted, most of his followers deserted him although some, who also became Moslems, believed his action was to operate inside the Islamic state for the benefit of the Jewish people. The result was that Kabbalah was forbidden to be studied and practised except by men over forty, married and learned. This meant that Kabbalah was no longer part of general Jewish culture in case it might be misused again.

In Eastern Europe, where the Cossack massacres of the 17th century had devastated a seemingly secure Jewish community, there was an atmosphere of total despair. It seemed that what Luria had said about the shattering of Worlds was indeed true. What made things yet more difficult was that the rabbis had no explanation for the disaster that had happened. They retreated into their study houses and debated about Talmudic regulations as a way of avoiding a harsh reality. The mass of Jews who had served as the middle class intermediaries between the Christian nobility and the peasantry were left in a state of deep economic and spiritual depression.

Providence met this situation by sending a remarkable old soul to lift up this community on the edge of losing its faith. The birth of Israel ben Eliezar was announced, according to legend, by Elijah to

Shabbethai Ẓebi Enthroned.
(From the title-page of " Tiḳḳun," Amsterdam, 1666.)

Figure 53—DELUSION

A classic case of abuse of higher knowledge was that of Shabbetai Zvi. He was a charismatic manic depressive psychotic who set himself up as the Messiah who would return the Jews to their Promised Land. He was supported by his John the Baptist, Nathan of Gaza, who used Kabbalistic terms to reinforce and enhance Shabbetai's claim. Many Jews, desolated by the Spanish expulsion and even worse bloody persecutions in the Ukraine, were taken in. Here, Shabbetai is seated upon the Throne of Solomon, being adored by his adherents. All this was to come to a sudden end when he became, under the threat of death, a Moslem. (Woodcut, 17th century.)

Figure 54—HASSIDISM
The once prosperous Polish Jewish community had been massacred by a Cossack
uprising against their Polish overlords. The Jews, as the middle class, had been
reduced not only to dire poverty but also spiritual doubt that they were special to
God. In the midst of this collective gloom arose the Kabbalistic master, the Baal
Shem Tov, who taught people to see the Divine in everyday life and enjoy all the
things they had taken for granted. Out of this view of raising one's level of
perception came a school of teachers who told enlightening stories rather than
debating law. Here a Hassidic rabbi dances at a wedding. (Beaten copper relief,
19th century.)

Figure 55—MESSIAH

Throughout all their suffering, the Jews waited for the Messiah to come. However, all the claimants down the centuries had failed to lead them back to Jerusalem. The Kabbalistic view was that the Messiah was a spiritual role passed on to different individuals over the generations. They were at the head of the spiritual hierarchy of their time. It was said that there were thirty-six righteous people who held the world in balance but they were but one stratum within a pyramid of highly evolved individuals. However, tradition stated that at the End of Days, Elijah would lead the last of the Messiahs into Jerusalem on a donkey as humanity reached an evolutionary culmination. (Passover Haggadah, 17th century.)

his parents in the town of Okop, in the Ukraine, around 1700 CE. As a young man he spent more time in meditation in the forest than in the synagogue although it is said that he studied Kabbalah there at night. When he was ready, he began to heal and teach in an informal way. Such was his wisdom and power that he soon gained the title of *Baal Shem Tov* which means 'Master of the Good Name'. This title was traditionally given to miracle workers. His approach was to use everyday life as a practical method of recovery and reconnection with spirituality. He took the Lurianic idea of the Divine sparks being buried in matter and releasing them by action and devotion. He maintained that God could be found in every situation. This had such an immediate appeal that he soon had a large following, including some eminent local rabbis who recognised his quality of saintliness and Kabbalistic knowledge. It was clear to them that the Baal Shem was indeed a great master, despite his humble attitude and homely ways. Unfortunately, the rabbinic establishment and even the famous scholar, the Gaon of Vilna, refused to recognise what became the Hassidic movement because it did not conform to their version of tradition.

This was not unusual as great mystics of every religion have often threatened the power of an established clergy that refuses to change. The alternative is to start a new movement based upon esoteric principles that have been buried beneath crystallised rituals, prayers and ideas. To bring about a spiritual revival required someone of the Baal Shem's calibre. Such individuals, according to Kabbalah, belong to the largely hidden company of thirty-six holy people. This is but one level of a spiritual pyramid headed by the current Messiah who is usually quite unknown but is well acquainted with what is going on below on Earth and in the Worlds above.

The Messiah, or the Anointed, is an embodied individual who holds the position for a certain time. In Islam they are called the Axis of the Age. Others might regard them as the Buddha of a period. In Kabbalah there is a chain of Messiahs including Moses, Joshua, David and Solomon. A rabbi once was asked where the present Messiah was. The reply was, 'Look among the beggars of Rome'. There is the story of the Baal Shem who was on a journey with a student. In a remote forest he stopped by a cottage and conversed, clearly very deeply, with an old man. The student, intrigued by his teacher's obvious respect, asked as they moved on who this person was. The reply came, 'The Messiah'.

Figure 56—EMANCIPATION
As a result of the Age of Reason which occurred in the 18th century, in Europe the Jews began to be freed from many medieval restrictions. They started to participate in the mainstream of Western civilisation. For example, Moses Mendelssohn, a philosopher and scholar, was accepted into cultured society. Here he is seen conversing with Gotthold Lessing, a German writer who based a play on him, called Nathan the Wise. *One result, however, of this emancipation was that Kabbalah became increasingly regarded as a religious superstition. In time, many Western educated Jews discarded their esoteric tradition as science and Reason became the fashion.* (Etching of Mendelssohn and Lessing, 18th century.)

In the 19th century, with the emancipation of Western European Jews, came a different kind of scholar. These were modern educated people who saw Kabbalah as an interesting but quaint form of ancient and medieval theology. While hundreds of texts were translated and examined, the spirit of the European so-called Enlightenment meant that the mystical element was regarded as a cultural delusion, not a reality in its own right. By the 20th century there was a whole body of scholarly studies on the subject but there was little differentiation between genuine material based upon real experience and learned opinion and superstition. Kabbalah was seen as no more than a religious phenomenon of another age. It only remained alive among the ultra-orthodox rabbis, distant oriental Jewish communities and a few Westerners interested in the Occult.

Fortunately, with the arising of the so-called 'New Age' movement in the aftermath of the Second World War there was a real search for spirituality. This was because Church and Synagogue were no longer schools of the soul. Young Western people looked to Sufism, Buddhism and other traditions, including the occult, to find the meaning of life on Earth after such a gruesome war. Many people, including Jews, found, to their surprise, that Kabbalah had answers to their questions and yearnings. Out of this arose meaningful translations of old texts, many books with a deeper understanding of Kabbalah when set out in contemporary psychological and scientific terms. These were integrated, like Neo-Platonism had been in the Middle Ages, into a modern version of this ancient mystical tradition. What follows is a brief account of the emerging new formulation that draws upon many sources.

Figure 57—ORIGINS
This diagram sets out the Kabbalistic understanding of the beginning of Existence. The topmost word, AYN, means NO-THING-NESS while the two words below, AYN SOF, mean ENDLESS-NESS. The circle of fire represents the Will of the Absolute that separates the relative universe from the Godhead. Within the sphere, which has been generated by the HOLY ONE withdrawing to allow a void to appear, are the ten emanations of the Sefirot. This action of the Absolute called forth a cosmic mirror to emerge by which God could behold God.
(Design by Prof James Russell, 20th century.)

6. *Macrocosm*

As has previously been noted, the key idea in Kabbalah is that God wishes to behold God. In order for this to come to pass, there has to be a mirror. This is accomplished by the manifestation of Existence out of non-Existence. The medieval Kabbalists had two terms for the Absolute who is beyond Existence. One was AYIN or NO-THING-NESS and the other was AYIN SOF or the LIMITLESS. According to tradition, a space had to be generated in order for Existence to come into being and so the Absolute withdrew into ITSELF so that a void could appear.

Into this space the AYIN SOF AUR, or the Will of the Absolute, emanated ten Divine principles that would govern the world. These Divine instruments, as they are sometimes called, unfolded in a specific pattern. From the first, called *Keter*, the Crown, came a second named *Hokhmah* or Wisdom, after which emerged its balancing complement, *Binah* or Understanding. Together they composed what was seen as the Supernal Triad. Seen metaphysically, Keter represented the source of all at the Place of Equilibrium while Hokhmah and Binah were the principles of initiation and pattern. In India, these three prime movers are known as Sattva, Rajas and Tamas. In China they are called the Tao, Yang and Yin. Together they are the heads of three columns that can be metaphysically defined as the central pillar of Grace, the right pillar of the Dynamic and the left pillar of Structure.

Immediately below this triad came what was known as the non- or invisible sefirah of *Daat* or Knowledge. This corresponds to a kind of 'black hole' or access point to what lies beyond. Here, it is said, the Will of the Absolute operates through this mystical veil to allow or disallow any process, up or down, to proceed. It is also seen as the pause or first interval in the Prime Octave which is about to continue.

The seven lower sefirot unfold in sequence down the Tree. The first of these, *Hesed* or Mercy and *Gevurah* or Judgement, can be seen as the principles of expansion and contraction besides being the equivalent to Divine emotion. The supernal opposites, in contrast, of Hokhmah

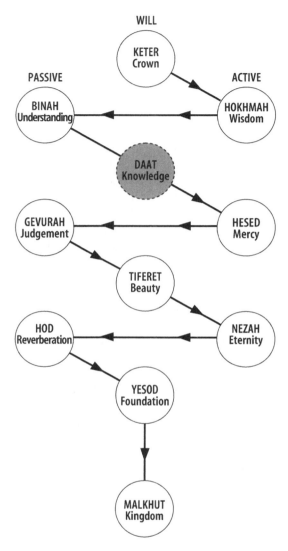

Figure 58—LIGHTNING FLASH
Here is seen the octave of Divine influx that follows a distinct pattern. At the top is the head of the column of equilibrium while to each side are the pillars of dynamic and structure. While these define the levels of Divine Mind, Morality and Action, the central sefirot mark out degrees of closeness to the Crown of their Source. This scheme is the prime metaphysical system that underlies the paths and triads that govern Existence. Indeed, each lower World takes on the laws of those above, making the lowest of materiality the most complex. (Halevi.)

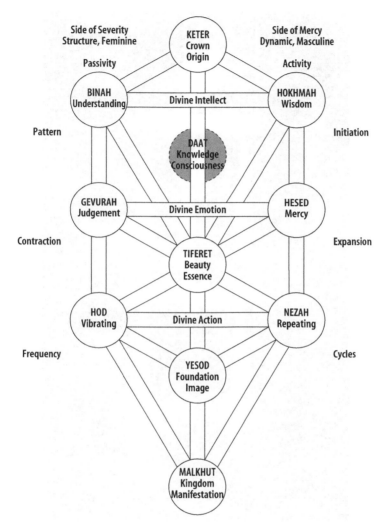

Figure 59—SCHEMA
Here the Biblical definitions are seen in philosophical and scientific terms. These enable us to perceive the forces and processes that allow Existence to function within certain limits in each of the four Worlds to come into being. Thus the same principle applies to galaxies, the Solar system and the human psyche and body, as well as to organisations and machines. By comprehending this basic model we are able to understand the workings of many things, great and small; even Time. In this scheme, the left side is the Past and the right the Future while the centre represents the Eternal and the passing show of Now. Observing all this is the silent watcher of the Absolute. (Halevi.)

Figure 60—GLORY OF GOD
The early Kabbalists also saw the primordial World of the Sefirot composed of the Names of God or, as in this case, one in particular. YHVH formed, when positioned in a vertical mode, the image of Adam Kadmon, the fiery humanoid figure of Ezekiel's vision. This was because the Holy Title had four distinct levels and three pillars which correspond to the Tree of Life. The individual letters, moreover, defined the head, heart and organ of generation besides the side arm and leg configurations. This is the basis of the Shiur Komah, *the* Book of Measurement. *The vast figure was called the KAVOD, the GLORY, as it represented the Divine Adam, the perfect image of God.* (Halevi.)

Figure 61—EMANATION
Light has always been associated with Divinity. Its radiance precedes all
Creation. In human terms, a flash of inspiration must come before any idea or
form. In modern science the original Big Bang of pure fire is seen as emerging
out of NO-THING-NESS. At the material level the beginning of the physical universe
seems rapid and violent; but from a cosmic dimension it is as slow as a blossoming
flower. This is how Kabbalah and many other esoteric traditions describe the
start of Existence. Some traditions even go on to explain that it is but a cycle in
which the blossom will wither and return to NO-THING-NESS again. In
Kabbalah, this process is called a Shemittah. (Robert Fludd, 17th century.)

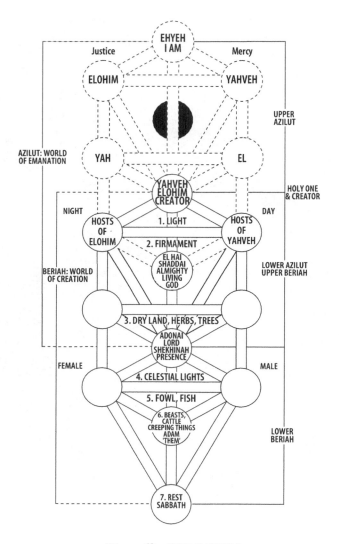

Figure 62—SEPARATION

The second World of Creation emerges out of that of Emanation. This begins at the heart of the Divine realm where the two Holy Names at the top of each side pillar combine to become YHVH ELOHIM, the Creator. EHYEH or I AM holds the centre and transmits the will of the Absolute to bring about Creation. From this combination come the seven levels defined by the seven Days spoken of in Genesis. This lower world is the equivalent of Plato's World of Ideas. In Kabbalah it is the dimension of the spirit, the essence of all that will come into being, as yet without form or substance. (Halevi.)

and Binah are viewed as the active and passive aspects of Divine intellect. Below, and in the centre of what will become the Tree of the sefirot, is *Tiferet* or Beauty. This is because it is the focus of the Tree's symmetry and holds the harmonious balance of all the functions and flows within the system. Here it is important to state that this Divine realm that is coming into being is not God but an expression of the Absolute.

The pair of sefirot beneath Tiferet are called *Nezah* and *Hod*, sometimes translated as Victory and Glory. These names are misleading. The root of the Hebrew word Nezah means 'Repetition', while Hod's root meaning is to 'Reverberate', like a peacock tail. These definitions are closer to their metaphysical functions. Nezah is the active principle of cycles that drive the many flywheels of Existence while the reverberations of Hod relate to the frequency on the scale of vibrations that pervade the universe. This is the level of Divine Action.

Yesod or Foundation is the second, lower interval in the descending octave of manifestation. It is the place where the image of what is coming into being appears. A parallel is the composition of a poem. First comes the will to write, then an idea may arise about, say, the vastness and depth of the night sky. This stimulates a profound emotion of awe as the music of the spheres is heard. The experience is then formulated in an eloquent image. This is the work of Yesod or Foundation just prior to the poem actually being written down. The end product is *Malkhut* or Kingdom, that is the completed operation. Malkhut is where all that is operating above comes to rest in full manifestation.

The twenty-two paths in between the sefirot facilitate a flow, in either direction, to generate different patterns within the Tree. For example, at the human level the path between Yesod (the ego) and Malkhut (the body) allows the mind to perceive the outer world according to its mood and receive any sensory impressions coming in. The paths also make up triads within the Tree of the psyche. Some, for example, act as the mental and instinctive functions; while others relate to the soul and spirit. This is because the human mind is based on the Tree of Life.

This primordial sefirotic Tree of Life generates what is called the Divine World of *Azilut* which means, in Hebrew, to be 'next to', in this case the Absolute. As such it is the direct reflection of the Absolute's Will. Some Kabbalists perceive it as a humanoid figure, as in Ezekiel's

Figure 63—MYTHOLOGY

The ancient world used poetic imagery to describe cosmic processes. Metaphysics had not yet developed to the point where it was a generally accepted language. This had to wait for the Greeks and their philosophical approach. Here are seen the creatures of the Air, Water and Land. As noted, the birds and fish represent the archangels and angels while the beasts of the Field are the archetypes for Earthly species. Note that they are always in pairs. The principle of incarnate consciousness is focused on the central column. This is imparted at birth and withdrawn at death, leaving the form and substance of a species inert. The body then returns to the four states of matter while the life principle of an earthly creature retreats back into the invisible World above. (Lutheran Bible, 16th century.)

Figure 64—PARADISE
Here in the Garden of Eden, each species of flora and fauna is seen in its perfection.
In this medieval print, the androgynous spiritual Adam has become divided into
the twin souls of Adam and Eve. They represent all humanity in what is called the
Treasure House of Souls. Between them is the Tree of Knowledge, entwined
around which is Satan the Tester while above and beyond is the Tree of Life.
These Trees represent, respectively, the Worlds of Creation and Emanation. After
the human couple had sinned they were sent down into the lowest world of
materiality because they were not yet mature enough to possess spiritual knowledge
or enter the Divine realm from where they originally came They had to lose their
innocence in order to gain experience in the course of the four journeys.
(Medieval woodcut.)

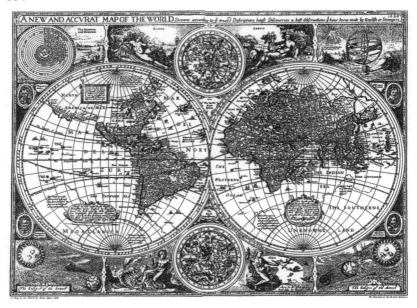

Figure 65—ELEMENTAL WORLD
*This physical dimension is composed of radiant, gaseous, fluid and solid states
of matter. In other words, Fire, Air, Water and Earth. As such they interact with
each other throughout the physical universe, stimulating myriads of forms and
processes that can be seen in minerals, plants and animals. The Earth existed for
millions of years without humanity; the Seven Days of Creation represent vast
epochs that define the progression of cosmic evolution. Only when the conditions
were right, in the sixth phase, was it possible for humanity to be incarnated by
taking on a primitive body. From then on, mankind has been slowly cycling
between the Treasure House of Souls and Earth through reincarnation. These
wheels of Life and Death are called, in Kabbalah, the* Gilgulim. *(Engraving, 17th
century)*

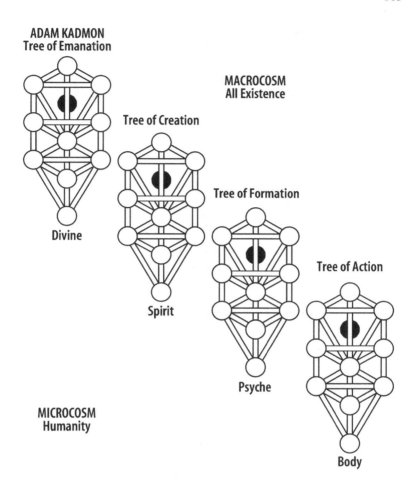

ADAM KADMON
Tree of Emanation

MACROCOSM
All Existence

Tree of Creation

Divine

Tree of Formation

Spirit

Tree of Action

Psyche

MICROCOSM
Humanity

Body

Figure 66—FOUR WORLDS
Here are shown the four Trees or sets of laws at each level. The lower face, as it is called, of one realm corresponds to the upper face of the world below. Here also is shown the macrocosmic dimension of the universe, and the microcosmic of humanity. This indicates that a developed individual can experience every domain whereas plants, animals, angels and demons can only exist on their particular plane. There is a Biblical saying that a human can go beyond the angels and also sink below the level of the beasts. Here is the factor of free will and its possibilities. Indeed, one person can become a human vegetable while another can be a Buddha or Maitreya. (Halevi.)

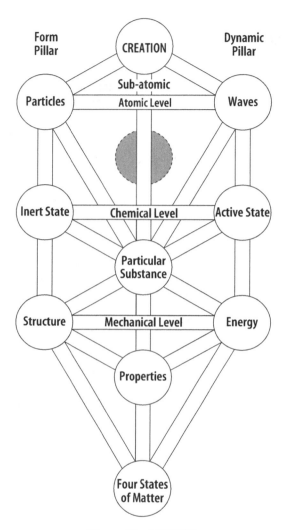

Figure 67—MATTER

In this Tree, the material realm is set out into its various sefirotic levels. It demonstrates how the physical world is ruled by Divine principle. Each order defines a specific process while the pillars show the relationship between structure and dynamic modes of materiality. Beyond the highest point of Creation lies what mundane science believes there is nothing it can detect. This does not mean that another reality is not there. Anyone with a degree of sensitivity can tell that there is a difference between the cleanness of virgin land and the sad feeling of an old battlefield. This cannot be measured at this point in time by any instrument. (Halevi.)

fiery vision. They called it Adam Kadmon, the initial outline of a SELF-portrait of the Godhead. Other Kabbalists call this Divine figure the *Kavod* or Glory of God. A vision of it was seen by Isaiah in the Temple, seated also upon a great throne. These are poetic and symbolic images that attempt to convey the majesty of the Divine realm.

This Realm of Light is the Eternal World of potentiality from which comes the second Airy universe of Creation. This corresponds to Plato's world of ideas. The spiritual process, described in great detail in the Book of Genesis, should be seen as an unfolding of Essences. On the first Day comes the spirit of Light, on the second Air, in the division of the spiritual Firmament. Then comes the division of the concepts of water from earth and life, symbolised by the appearance of the idea of plants. Then on the fourth Day comes the ordering of the four elements which, at this stage, are not yet in form or matter. A human parallel would be Shakespeare's *Hamlet* before he worked out the plot or put pen to paper. The same is true for Existence which, at this point, is a developing scenario in the Mind of God.

On the fifth Day came the 'Fowl of the Air' and the 'Fish of the Sea'—that is, a symbolic way of describing the spirits of the archangels and angels. They were followed, on the sixth Day, by the creation of the 'Beasts of the Field' or those creatures that would eventually inhabit the Planet Earth when it came into being. These lowest of physical beings were archetypes of every animal. For example, the vertebrates—fish, reptiles and mammals—were all to have some kind of skeleton. On that same Day the spiritual Adam appeared as the being that encompassed all that had been created. The Seventh Day of Sabbath completed the octave. The World of Creation or, in Hebrew, *Beriah* is cosmic in quality and quantity. It is vast and entirely invisible except in the imagination or in a vision. It is the powerhouse of Existence, the breath of Life or *Ruah Hakodesh*, the Holy Spirit.

The next World of Formation or Paradise is where essences take on shapes. The Idea of the Rose becomes manifest in many forms, as does the Spirit of the Cat. This multiplicity of forms makes the Garden of Eden a Paradise in its perfect beauty and variety. Everything is in its prime in this Watery World where the entire life cycle can be viewed simultaneously. It is here that people who have just died review their lives in a series of intense memories that will be a self-assessment of their performance.

Below this World of *Yetzirah*, which will also contain Hell as well

108

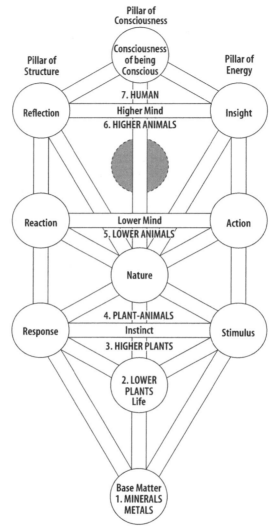

Figure 68—EVOLUTION
Darwin's theory in no way conflicts with Divine Law. Indeed, as can be seen, it concurs with a natural progression. Moreover, each level has a particular way of relating to the environment. Below the human triad, all creatures are more or less programmed by evolution to react in a certain way while humans have the option of rising above their instincts. Moreover, while all animals are very conscious of the immediate, a human being can be conscious of being conscious, consider the past and future and project into the macroscopic and microscopic realms through imagination. (Halevi.)

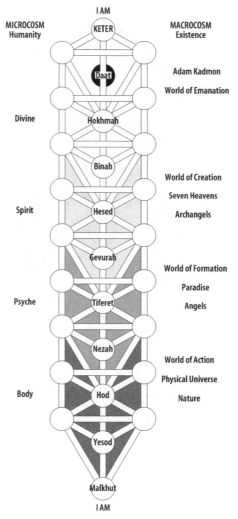

Figure 69—CHAIN OF BEING
When all the worlds are interlocked the Great Tree becomes apparent; so too
does the way in which the four Trees interlock with each other. Also to be seen is
the relationship between the microcosm of a human being and the macrocosm of
the various universes. This complex but intricate system of Existence is embodied
in the Hebrew word ASHER or THAT which is held between the I AM above and
the I AM below; that is, beyond the ultimate Keter, the Crown, and Malkhut, the
Kingdom. As such, Existence will remain in being as long as the HOLY ONE
wills it. The vertical Sefirot are quite different in that they are to do with degrees
of consciousness. (Halevi.)

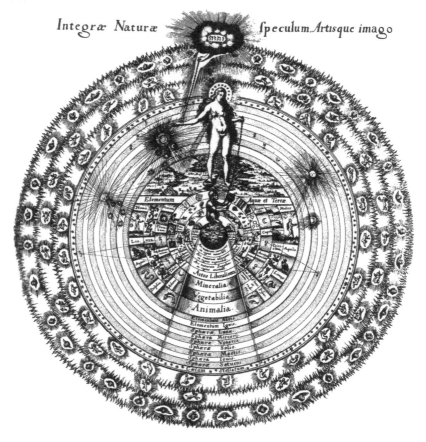

Figure 70—MIRROR OF EXISTENCE

The engraved word 'speculum' refers, in this 17th century Rosicrucian-Kabbalistic print, to the idea that God wishes to behold God through the Mirror of Existence which emanates from the cloud YHVH. The three outer circles represent the higher worlds of the Divine, Creation and Formation with their angelic inhabitants. The physical realm begins with the stars, the Solar system and the Earth with its various levels of organic beings. At the centre are the different human activities with the monkey mind of undeveloped man seeking to measure the immeasurable. The woman connecting all the worlds is a Rosicrucian version of the Shekhinah, *the Divine Feminine.* (Robert Fludd, 17th century.)

as Paradise, comes the realm of physical manifestation; that is, solids, liquids, gases and radiation that compose the material universe. This cosmos manifests only in the ever-moving Now as the evolution of Existence unfolds. From the galaxies to the subatomic particles, physical Time is ordered into past, present and future. Below this basic matrix is the NO-THING-NESS of God. This bottom-most universe makes up the last rung of Jacob's Ladder. What holds all four worlds together is called the *Kav* or the vertical line that stretches from the highest to the lowest levels and forms the spine of what is known as the fifth and 'Great Tree' that interlocks all the universe. In this Kabbalistic system there is the overlapping of the upper and lower faces of each World that comprises Jacob's Ladder. Such an arrangement enables different realities to interconnect. This feature is symbolically described in Kabbalistic texts as a chain of shells and nut kernels or a series of skulls and brains, one inside the other. The scheme is geometrically set out in Figures 45 and 69.

An example of how an upper and lower face interact is to be seen in how the physical reflects the psychological in body language. Over time, some postures become permanent and reveal much about the person's temperament. Likewise, a disciplined form of body yoga can train the mind to be more active or passive. This works upon the ancient esoteric principle of 'As above, so below'. The Kabbalistic art of reading faces is based upon this premise.

It is said that there were several other Existences before the present one came into being. They were, according to Jewish myth, part of a vast process in that each one was a stage of a huge cosmic cycle or *Shemittah*. The current one is said to be that of Gevurah or Judgement which corresponds to the Hindu version of an epoch of Severity. The end of the total cycle will be when the Epoch of Keter the Crown is reached. This will occur, according to tradition, on the Day of Resurrection when all humanity returns, each to their own place, in the vast being of Adam Kadmon. Our mission, as the human microcosm of the Divine, is to bring back all our experience so as to transform the sketched outline of Adam Kadmon into a full and complete SELF-portrait of the Absolute as viewed in the Mirror of Existence.

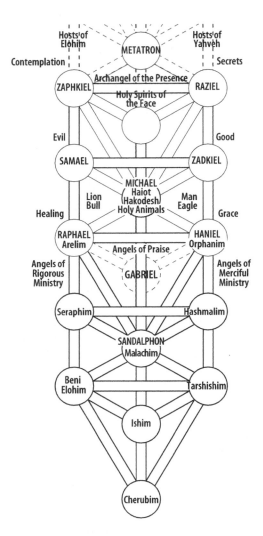

Figure 71—ANGELICS

*The upper Tree is that of Creation or the World of the Spirit. This is inhabited by
the archangels. These are the captains of the lower hosts of angels. Each name
has a specific meaning; Zaphkiel contemplates God; Raziel has God's secrets,
while Samael and Zadkiel are concerned with punishment and reward. Raphael
is God's Healer and Haniel God's Grace. Great Michael commands the Hosts
while Gabriel guards the Gates of Heaven. The angelics act according to their
sefirotic functions. Metatron and Sandalphon are alternate names for Enoch in
specific roles. (Halevi.)*

7. *Supernatural*

The Holy Names of God have a particular meaning when set upon the Tree of Emanation. At the Crown is EHYEH, I AM. Just below, at the top of the right hand column, is that of YAHVEH, which is related to the Merciful aspect of Divinity, while at the head of the left column is ELOHIM or the Just side of the Divine. There has, however, been some debate about their significance. What can be said is that YAHVEH is essentially active, the Divine principle that executes the Will of EHYEH while ELOHIM, a plural term, indicates a process of Divine differentiation. Here it must be remembered that the Divine is but an expression of the Absolute. A human parallel would be when a painter first makes an outline of a self-portrait but has, as yet, to fill in the detail. In *The Zohar* it says, 'And Face did not yet gaze upon Face until Existence came into being in all its Glory.

EL and YAH define, again in artistic terms, the broad laying in of the composition and then the tightening up of the image to bring it closer to the precise character of the sitter. The combined Name, YAHVEH ELOHIM, at the Tiferet of Azilut is God the Creator who, as the principle of creativity, adds a particular quality to the picture. Consider the difference between a Rembrandt and a Van Gogh portrait. The hosts of YAHVEH ELOHIM are the equivalent to the vitality and detail of the portrait with EL HAI SHADDAI or LIVING ALMIGHTY bringing life to the painting. The lowest place, at the human level, is the fabric being painted upon and the various pigments. In the case of the Divine, it is the substance of Existence. This bottom-most position has the Divine Name of ADONAI or MY LORD appended to it.

Out of the place of the CREATOR emerges the Crown of the Tree of Creation. From there the Seven Halls of Heaven will come. The upper portion of this sequence relates to the lower part of the Divine Tree. The two highest levels in this Creative realm are where Enoch, alias Metatron, and the Great Holy Council reside. Below them come the lesser degrees of spirituality occupied by two ranks of saints and

Figure 72—HOLY CREATURES
These vast beings represent the four worlds. The Man is the symbol of the Divine;
the Eagle, the Airy dimension of the Spirit while the Lion's heart represents the
Watery and emotional level of the soul. The Bull's heavy mass denotes the weight
and solidity of the Earthy world. These creatures are said to hover around the
Heavenly Throne. Their origin comes from Ezekiel's vision and were later to be
used as symbols for the four Christian Gospels. Here it must be remembered that
Jesus (or Joshua ben Miriam) and all his disciples were Jews and familiar with
Kabbalah, although it was not known by this name at the time. (Book of Kells,
9th century.)

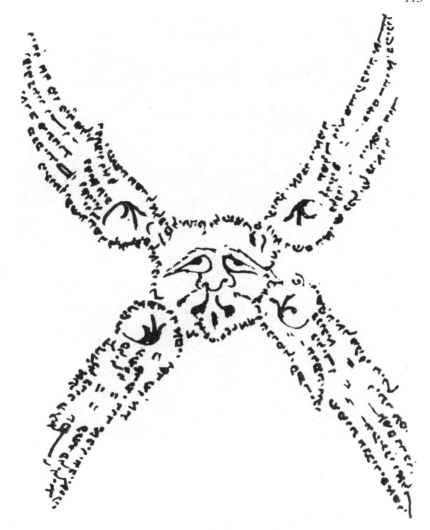

Figure 73—ANGEL
In this image made of Hebrew words, the rank of an angelic is to be judged by
the number of its wings. These not only denote status but that they are not creatures
of the Earth. Each one of these celestial beings had a specific task that was
written on its forehead. These names were symbolic of its cosmic function, from
galactic monitors to making snowflakes. They operated according to particular
physical, moral and spiritual conditions. Heathens and Pagans called them
nature spirits or lesser and greater gods. The Jews saw them as just servants of
the Absolute. (Medieval manuscript.)

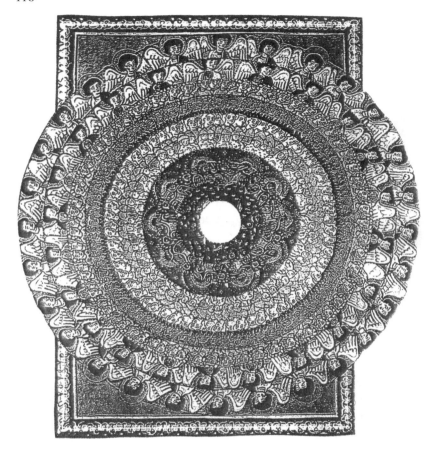

Figure 74—HEAVENLY HOSTS
In this medieval vision the order of the angelics is clearly set out in its ranks.
Those closer to the centre, the entrance to the Divine realm, are archangels while
the angels are at the edge, furthest from the Light. The angelics have to be held
in their position as it is their automatic inclination to assert their particular
function. This is checked by its opposite number on the angelic Tree while those
celestial beings on the central column keep the equilibrium. The demonics are
called the Kellippot, the Shells. They operate at the extremities of structure and
dynamic, where they seek to disrupt the order of Existence through any excess.
(Hildegard of Bingen, 11th century.)

sages, the saints being active and the sages being reflective roles of teachers.

When Enoch was transfigured by fire—that is, Divinity—into a human being with archangelic powers, he filled the place vacated by the rebellious Lucifer. As Metatron, he was given authority over all the angelics as he bore the Name of God, indicating that he was fully Self-realised. Below and on either side are the archangels Raziel and Zaphkiel. Their function, according to their names, is to reveal the secrets of the Holy One to mystics and aid in the contemplation of them. Prophets would experience their presence in moments of revelation while philosophers recognise their supernatural assistance in a profound moment of thought.

The same is true for the archangelic principles symbolised by Zadkiel and Samael. The former is concerned, for example, with the principle of reward and the latter with punishment. Good and evil are associated with these two archangelics but it would be better to define these spiritual factors as cosmic creation and destruction or the processes of integration and disintegration. These are an integral part of the evolution of the universe, life and death. Righteousness and maliciousness would be the parallel of the human spiritual level.

Raphael and Haniel, which can be translated as the Healer of God and God's Grace, represent the spiritual processes of mending what has been damaged and giving it the power to function again. Here the term Grace can be likened to the feeling of vitality returning after being ill. Together, these two archangels head the side columns of the lower World of Formation. They govern the lesser angelics below, known by the general title of the Hosts of YAHVEH and ELOHIM.

Gabriel means the Warrior of God. This celestial being guards the Yesod or Foundation of the second Heaven. This corresponds, as we shall see, to the Daat or place of direct mystical knowledge in the human psyche. Gabriel also makes sure that nothing too powerful bursts into the lower Worlds of incarnate humanity and Nature. When it is permitted, it is called a miracle. A classic example is the parting of the Red Sea by the rising of a great wind, a symbol of the *Ruah Hakodesh*, the Holy Spirit, that blew back the waters. Here a natural order was adjusted by cosmic forces to get a miraculous result.

The archangel Michael holds the central position of co-ordination in the Tree of Creation. This great being is the Commander in Chief of all the Heavenly hosts who controls the tendency of each angelic role which seeks to rule or resist others from different pillars and

Figure 75—MISSION

Here an army of angels sets out to execute a specific task. It might be to correct an imbalance in the cosmos by defeating Satan's battalions who feed off disorder. This process is seen in Nature when the weather, for example, is excessively violent. This is contained by cosmic forces, seen as gods by the ancients. The battles between the planetary angels, when they were in inharmonious configurations, were believed to disrupt the world of humans and bring about war and disaster. In occult Kabbalah, the angelics were seen as entities that could be employed. However such beings, like all professionals, have to be paid which most magicians forget and are therefore in their debt. This is why magical operations are forbidden. (Doré, 19th century.)

Figure 76—GREAT MICHAEL
This great angelic being occupies a special position, in the place on Jacob's Ladder where the three upper Worlds meet. Here is the lowest sefirah of the Divine where the Shekhinah, or Holy Presence, resides and the centre of the World of Spirit is found. This is also where the highest sefirah of the World of Formation is located. It is also the position of the Heavenly Jerusalem where the most evolved of humanity reside when they are discarnate, although very advanced individuals may visit it. Michael guards this nexus which is the Heart of the Heavenly Throne. (Byzantine, 13th century.)

Figure 77—HUMAN ANGELS

The Hebrew word for angel simply means messenger. Here the long-dead Roman poet, Virgil, guides Dante through what might be seen as a Dark Night of the Soul. In Kabbalah, such discarnate teachers are known as the maggidim. Their task is to guide and protect those on the path, especially when the going is tough or frightening. They are called, by other cultures, guardian angels, the ancestors or fairy godmothers. They may be just a warning voice or even appear to be quite solid. After they have delivered their message or carried out their mission, they vanish. (Doré's illustration for Dante's *Divine Comedy,* 19th century.)

levels. Michael's function is also to maintain the balance between the upper and lower Worlds of Creation and Formation. The name Michael means 'Like unto God'. The position this Captain of the Hosts holds is where the three Higher Worlds meet. Above Michael's position reside what are called the Holy Spirits of the Face while below, also centred on the Middle Column, are the 'Angelics of Praise'. To the left, on the pillar of structure and right, the dynamic pillar, are those called the 'Angels of Ministry' which are concerned with the functions of Justice and Mercy and the administrators of cosmic action and reaction. The laws of 'Measure for measure' or karma come under their jurisdiction.

Sandalphon, at the foot of the Tree of Creation, is another name for Enoch. It is said that Sandalphon is not an angel because the Name does not have El within it, signifying free will. His role is to transmit conscious or sincere prayers, in contrast to the millions of petitions and praises ritually offered up each day as a matter of routine. Indeed, it is quite rare for such an event. It can only occur when the person praying is in what is called the *Gadlut* state of 'being conscious of being conscious', in contrast to the *Katnut* or lesser condition. This means merely speaking the words without being aware of what is actually being said. Sandalphon recognises the difference; like a gull knowing its own chick's call amid a huge flock, he picks the prayer up and carries it to the highest Heaven. Tradition says Sandalphon is the tallest of the Heavenly Hosts, meaning he can operate throughout Jacob's Ladder.

The four Holy Animals, as they are called, which hover around the Throne of Heaven represent the four Worlds. The Man symbolises the Divine realm of Adam Kadmon; the Eagle, the Airy world of the Spirit or Creation; the Lion, the icon of courage or heart, relates to the watery World of Formation; while the Bull is the symbol of the Earth. In the same area of Jacob's Ladder where these vast creatures hover is the celestial Jerusalem where the current Messiah is said to reside. Whoever this may be is incarnate but fully cognisant of the Higher realms. He or she is responsible, at that point in history, for the spiritual life and evolution of humanity. They watch over the course of events first-hand and pass on intelligence to the Holy community. Periods of calm, times of destruction and epochs of creativity are partly dependent upon the state and movements of the cosmos and direct observation of mankind's reaction is vital. Moreover, no civilisation could arise without the presence of such a highly developed human being who

Figure 78—INSTRUCTION
Here Dante is being taught by a maggid of a very high order. He is being shown
one of the celestial levels with its host of angels. This relates to the ancient
Merkabah tradition. There is good reason to believe that Dante, who had Jewish
friends, was not unfamiliar with the rabbinic descriptions of Hell, Paradise and
Heaven. Included in these texts were observations about the Solar system and
astrology. (Doré's illustration for Dante's *Divine Comedy,* 19th century.)

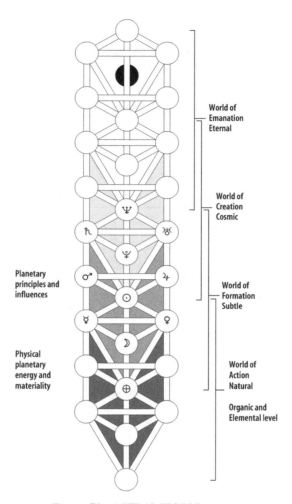

World of
Emanation
Eternal

World of
Creation
Cosmic

Planetary
principles and
influences

World of
Formation
Subtle

Physical
planetary
energy and
materiality

World of
Action
Natural

Organic and
Elemental level

Figure 79—ASTRAL WORLD
This term refers to the realm of Formation, or that of the psyche. Kabbalists related
this to the Treasure House of Souls where the fate of each individual is determined
after death and before birth, according to merit. Centuries of observation going
back to Abraham indicates that the celestial bodies and their positions in the
zodiac indicated that a person's life was set, to a degree, by their birth chart. The
planets and the Moon were considered to be angels while the Sun was seen as an
archangel. The latter two certainly influenced life on Earth, through the amount
of light and the rhythm of the tides and plant growth. Over the centuries the effect
of the planets was observed. For example, individuals with a strong Mars were
noted to be courageous while a strong Saturn encouraged caution. These factors
generated a particular temperament and therefore fate. (Halevi.)

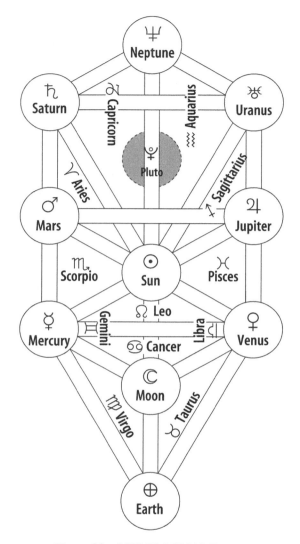

Figure 80—ASTROLOGICAL TREE
*While Jews were forbidden to worship the celestial gods they could, like
Abraham, be astrologers. Hence the correspondence between the Tree and the
Solar system. Here, the zodiac is also ascribed to various triads, according to
their rulers. For example, Mercury is the governor of Gemini and Virgo. Over
recent centuries, the newly discovered outer planets have replaced the ancient
nominations of the zodiac and Milky Way. Kabbalists, like other branches of
knowledge, always added new discoveries when they filled the scheme. Pluto, for
example, is the gateway to beyond the Solar system. (Oral tradition.)*

heads an incarnate spiritual hierarchy on Earth. These are old souls who stimulate evolution wherever they are stationed. Without such people, humanity would still be a savage and barbaric society. There would be no morality, profound thought, great art or science.

The angelic names that are ended with 'im' rather than 'el' indicate that they are composite, not individual entities. These hosts of lesser angels are in charge of such minor functions as manufacturing snowflakes, maintaining galaxies or watching over different species of animals. As such, they are organised into regiments of the left and right of the Trees of Formation and Action. There are myriads of them with local commanders at every level. The early rabbis used the Roman Army as a model to describe different orders of these supernatural beings because it defined, in intelligible terms, the chain of command in the Higher domains.

At the physical level, the Solar system was seen by some Kabbalists as a great celestial being. Within it, the Sun was regarded as a minor archangel because it was radiant, in contrast to the angels of the Moon and planets which reflected its light. By the Middle Ages astrology, which was practised by many rabbis, had given each heavenly body a well-defined character. These were related to the Sefirotic Tree because they matched so well. For example, the Sun seemed to fit perfectly with the central position of Tiferet, the Self; while the ever-changing Moon clearly related to Yesod, the ordinary mind. Malkhut was obviously the place of the Earth or body; with Mercury and Venus respectively at Hod and Nezah, the bio-psychological functions. Mars' characteristics clearly put it in the position of Gevurah which means controlled 'power' while Jupiter, the expansive planet, obviously occupied the place of Hesed. These two with the Sun related to the soul triad. Saturn, positioned at Binah, again seemingly corresponded to the intellectual qualities found in the sefirah of Understanding.

The other planets of Uranus, Neptune and Pluto were unknown at that time and so the Milky Way was put in the place of Hokhmah while Keter was seen as the celestial sphere that contained them all. By the 20th century the outer planets had been discovered. Their astrological characteristics were based upon years of observation which enabled Kabbalists to position Uranus in Hokhmah, the sefirah of intellectual revelation and inspiration. Neptune appeared to have a connection with the Divine as the ruler of Pisces, the sign of mystics, and so was related to Keter while Pluto, which is half in and half out

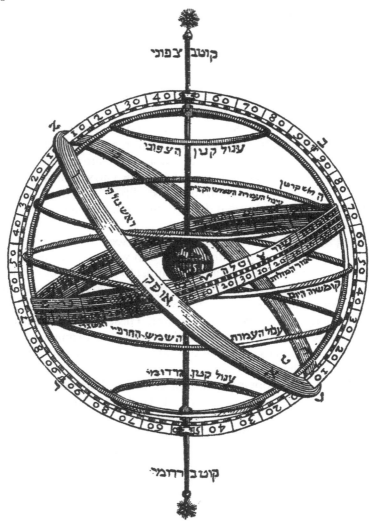

Figure 81—ARMILLARY SPHERE

In the middle ages the Jews played an important role in developing astrology. Besides inventing new instruments and calculating more accurately the way the macrocosm might influence the microcosm, they debated fiercely about free will. Was fate fixed? If so, it meant that there was no choice. If this was the case there was no point to the Commandments, as the evil or good person had no possibility of being anything else. This meant reward and punishment in this life or the next world. For those who believed in reincarnation, the next 'Life' was a solution that explained why the good suffer and the bad might prosper, due to karma. (Tobias Cohen, 18th century.)

of the Solar system, was placed in Daat. The reason for this is that it was the door between the Solar system and what lay beyond.

There were also the demonic aspects of Existence to consider. Some medieval Kabbalists maintained that each sefirah had a dark side. These took on, for example, the negative facets of Gevurah and Hesed. The former, in excess, precipitates a crushing form of destruction while a demonic Hesed explodes things beyond their proper limitations. In human affairs these evil aspects are observed in depression and mania. As regards Binah and Hokhmah, the negative side of Understanding becomes the ultimate clever bigot while Wisdom turns into the insane genius. The dark side of Tiferet is brilliant but inflated self-importance, as can be seen in Napoleon; while a distorted Yesod produces, in ordinary people, a disordered routine and chaos. The sinister side of Malkhut is serious physical illness.

However, even the Tree of Evil, as it was called—presided over by Satan, Kabbalists believed—has its cosmic function. As one sage observed, no one knows how holy they really are until their saintly feathers have been ruffled by a Lucific test or disruptive event. It was also noted that each of the seven lower sefirot had a sin related to it. A wicked Malkhut generated covetousness, Yesod, false witness; while Hod encouraged stealing and Nezah, adultery. A bad Tiferet stimulated the sin of pride, while Gevurah permitted excess anger and Hesed, envy. The sins of the highest sefirot were beyond most people. Only those who had reached an advanced degree of development had to face the temptations of thinking that they understood everything, believed their false prophecies or were able to perform miracles. The sin of Keter was to be convinced that one was the Messiah. Not a few mystics have fallen for this temptation. Every mental institution has at least one inmate who believes they are the Anointed or even God.

128

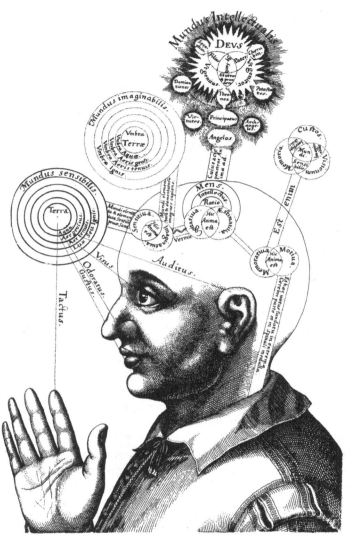

Figure 82—INNER UNIVERSE
It was believed that if a human being was a microcosm of Existence then there
must be, within each person, the equivalent of the four Worlds. These could be
defined as the physical, psychological, spiritual and Divine levels of an individual.
In this engraving, the body is clearly the material vehicle but the two lower circles
are not accurate in their definition, in that they do not convey the qualities of the
soul and spirit. This is probably due to a distortion of the Teaching, although it
is clear the Tree at the top is Kabbalistic in origin. This diagram is an amalgam
of various traditions. (Robert Fludd, 17th century.)

8. Microcosm

According to Kabbalah, a human being is a minute version of the universe. Moreover, that humanity's origins are to be found within the being of Adam Kadmon, the vast humanoid figure of fire that symbolises the realm of Emanation. It is said that each individual is a spark of light that comes from a specific part of Adam. Seen another way, we may be likened to cells inside a particular organ or limb. This means that each of us has a special function within the universal scheme. Another more metaphysical way of describing our place in Adam Kadmon is to see it in terms of the Tree of Life diagram. For example, a human photon of consciousness may originate from the left or right pillar, be closely associated with a particular sefirah, path or triad. Thus a position metaphorically in, say, the brain or thumb would define what a person's destiny might be when they attain a conscious degree of Self-realisation. This is what Kabbalah is all about. The process, however, takes a long time and many trials and tests over numerous lives.

In the first of the four Great journeys, a human Divine spark is required to make the descent into the world of Creation where it, and its associate companions, are initially enclothed in Spirit. Unlike the angelics, demonics and all the terrestrial entities, humanity was not created but inserted, on the Sixth Day, in the form of an androgynous Spiritual Adam, into the World of Time and Space. This set in motion a vast operation that would only terminate at the end of Existence. In this spiritual dimension the human masculine and feminine aspects are still, as yet, undifferentiated; 'Male and Female Created He them', says the Bible. By this is meant that they were as yet without a form or body. These would come later, as humanity was to be the vehicle by which God could behold God at every level. This meant that mankind would experience all realities from the atomic basis of physical existence to the ultimate height of Divine consciousness. Such is possible because a human being is capable not only of being conscious of being conscious but also to enter and operate in all the Worlds. This

Figure 83—TREASURE HOUSE OF SOULS
Prior to birth and after death, most human beings reside in one of the paradises.
Here they are in an ethereal form which is as substantial, in this subtle world, as
the body is on Earth. It is said that there is a finite number of souls who are
related by group function and karma. Some are specialists and others generalists,
like the cells of the body, but many are also connected by being soul mates or
having unfinished business from previous lives. Since early history the numbers
on Earth have increased as more young souls have come down to begin their
Journey of development. (Doré's illustration for Dante's *Divine Comedy*, 19th
century.)

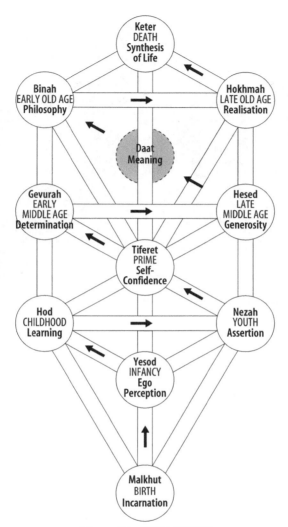

Figure 84—LIFE CYCLE

As can be seen, the passage between birth and death follows the Lightning Flash down and up the Tree. Each embryonic phase and life age corresponds to a stage of development. However, while all who complete life's physical journey may learn much, some fixate at a certain point and remain stuck at a place in their psychological evolution. Those who continue to mature go on to reach the upper levels of self-realisation and even attain understanding and wisdom. The most advanced souls go through the initiation of Daat and reach the Crown of enlightenment. They can then choose to leave the Wheel of Transmigration or return to Earth on the Third Journey of aiding those who want to develop. (Halevi.)

Figure 85—FOUR JOURNEYS

The first is that of the initial descent into the physical world in a state of innocence while the second is that of developing by experience. During these learning exercises individuals, by personal choice, can remain at the mineral level, achieving nothing but physical survival, while those who wish to live a pleasant life and have a family are seen as vegetable level people. The more ambitious, those who desire to be the best and dominate their field, are classified as animal people. Those who want to be fully human are usually individuals who are on the third journey of passing on what they have learned. The fourth journey is for those who have completed their earthly mission. However, they sometimes choose to descend to help in some large and important historic operation. (The four levels of humanity, Medieval woodcut.)

is something neither angel nor animal can do. They are limited to their particular level and area of operation. For example, an angel cannot take out a mortgage or an animal discover anti-matter.

However, in order to acquire such an overall degree of perception, each individual has to work for this capacity. While Self-realisation in humans is innate, it has to be developed. Included in this capacity is the asset of free will which means they can err by being too 'wilful' or too 'will-less'. It is only when a person is 'willing' to learn that they can be the Absolute's conscious agent. As the Bible then records, Adam having come down into the World of Formation, represented by the Garden of Eden, each human spirit divided into two. These soul mates, represented by Adam and Eve, had much to learn. The first lesson, as noted, was the temptation of doing what is forbidden. This was to teach them about the dangers of breaking universal law. Every action, they were to be taught, has a good or bad result; every effect is the result of a cause. This was a vital piece of information for when they would put on 'coats of skin', that is, when they were incarnated on Earth. Their organic bodies were to be the physical vehicles that enabled them, like a diving suit, to operate at the material level.

Paradise is called, by Kabbalah, the 'Treasure House of Souls'. There are, according to tradition, a finite number of human beings. On this non-physical plane, the soul mates are well aware of each other. However, they are not always incarnated at the same time or place as part of their education. This accounts for the very human preoccupation with finding one's soul mate. This theme recurs in folklore, literature and art. Modern psychology may speak about the Anima and Animus but the sudden, deep recognition or attraction between people is not just about resonating archetypes or sexual chemistry. It is also about meeting members of one's soul group, as we do not come down to incarnate alone. First, however, we have to learn how to relate and work with others before we meet our soul mate and begin on the advanced phase of becoming one in the Spirit.

Upon being born, a particular set of laws comes into play that determine our fate, that is the path and karma for that incarnation. Each person is allocated, at the moment of birth, not only the physical legacy of their parents and family but that of the nation into which they are born. Then there is the particular lesson they have to master so that they can move on. This is determined by their performance in previous lives. This may be a pleasant or unpleasant educational course. In favourable cases, someone with a musical talent will be

134

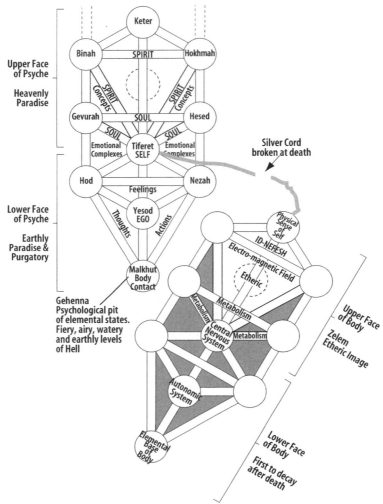

Upper Face of Psyche

Heavenly Paradise

Keter

Binah   SPIRIT   Hokhmah

SPIRIT Concepts   SPIRIT Concepts

Gevurah   SOUL   Hesed

SOUL   SOUL

Emotional Complexes   Tiferet SELF   Emotional Complexes

Silver Cord broken at death

Hod   Nezah

Feelings

Lower Face of Psyche

Thoughts   Yesod EGO   Actions

Physical Sense of Self

ID-NEFESH

Earthly Paradise & Purgatory

Malkhut Body Contact

Electro-magnetic Field

Etheric

Gehenna Psychological pit of elemental states. Fiery, airy, watery and earthly levels of Hell

Metabolism   Metabolism

Central Nervous System   Metabolism

Upper Face of Body

Zelem Etheric Image

Autonomic System

Elemental Base of Body

Lower Face of Body

First to decay after death

Figure 86—DEATH

Upon dying, the Tree of the psyche separates from that of the body. This, after a short while, goes into decay as the four elements begin to revert to their primal state. The Zelem, as Kabbalah calls the etheric, that normally connects the body to the psyche through the electronic field, does not disperse for several days. This means that the so-called 'dead' person can still relate to the physical realm. Indeed, their presence can be felt by some and even seen by especially sensitive people. The Earth-freed psyche now begins to review the memories of the life now past. It then goes through a cleansing process known to many traditions as Purgatory before it proceeds to the appropriate level of the invisible Worlds. Here it resides until it is ready for the prenatal condition of the next life. (Halevi.)

Figure 87—OUT OF THE BODY

Many who have experienced a near-death state describe floating in a void until they encounter a tunnel, at the end of which is a Paradisiacal scene. Here some deceased person known to them or a figure of Light tells them to return to Earth, as it is not yet their time. In many traditions, this latter brilliant being is identified with a great prophet, saint or sage. In Kabbalah it may be Elijah, depending on the spiritual attainment of the individual. In some cases, people get a glimpse of Gehenna (or Hell) which makes them change their ways when they return to the body. (Hieronymus Bosch, 16th century.)

Figure 88—REINCARNATION
The transmigration of the soul through many bodies is accepted in Kabbalah.
Observations over many generations and ancient texts and the visions of mystics
indicate one lifetime is not enough to become fully evolved. Some people, for
example, have memories of other lives and places. Others recognise strangers
they seem already to know well. Such phrases in the Jewish prayer book as,
'Quicken the dead', and 'the next world' can be applied to reincarnation.
However, the misconception that one can be reborn as a lion or fox is contrary
to the process of evolution. These are not to be taken literally but as symbolic
descriptions of an animal level person. (Photograph, Girl standing perhaps by her
own grave, 19th century.)

reborn into a family of musicians to further their career. In another situation, a corrupt soul may find itself incarnated into a criminal Mafia family. Young souls are generally born into a stable society where they need to learn the basic skill of life on Earth. This period might span a thousand years of living in simple conditions until they are ready to individuate.

This requires the process of transmigration to carry over, from life to life, all the experience required for their eventual destiny or purpose in the cosmos. From prehistoric times humanity has worked its way up from the level of the hunter-gatherer, through that of the farmer and trader to that of high urban culture. At first, souls are usually born into tribal clans and then more mature and complex societies, such as towns, cities and nations. Within this long progression, people can choose to remain at the vegetable level of just pleasant survival, become animal people who compete to be the most dominant person in their community or set out to become fully human and Self-realised.

At the vegetable stage, the individual does not count. In primitive societies, for example, only the roles of sex and age are relevant. These communities are usually ruled by strong or shrewd animal people and occasionally by wise, truly human men or women. The last are usually old souls who have incarnated to help things along. They are also there to introduce morality and knowledge, as most people would remain barbaric if they were not educated and given the means to evolve.

Development begins when animal level individuals no longer find satisfaction in worldly success. Something is lacking. They then begin to ask questions about the meaning of their life and seek information or a discipline that starts to awaken their soul. They then move quickly on in one lifetime or slowly over many, depending on what effort they put in. Most look to the great traditions of religion and philosophy for help. If they are ready, they encounter people who are already on the Path. Such advanced individuals can be of any race. They might be priests, scholars or lay people who follow any one of the ancient esoteric lines. Their appearance might be obvious, as in the case of a saint or sage, but very often they are seemingly quite ordinary people. These are members of the Companions of the Light, as they are sometimes called. They are always alert to recognise each other, like two people who are awake in a room of sleepers. At this level there is no sectarian difference arising from different cultures. As one great mystic observed, 'There is no religion higher than Truth'.

Figure 89—HEAVEN AND HELL
These are general terms for different states in the post-mortem period, before rebirth. Being disembodied means that the psyche is naked and cannot deny its true nature. According to psychic insights, bad people will share the same space as those like them, which must be very unpleasant, whereas good people will have delightful company. At the bottom level of Hell are the dregs of humanity, especially the master criminals, politicians and clergy who have been responsible for great cruelty. They can only be redeemed when they acknowledge what they have done and are filled with remorse. This escape from Hell is always an option.
(Marmion Hours, 15th century.)

Kabbalah has many hints and insights into the process of the *Gilgulim* or Wheels of Life and Death. The Hebrew prayer book speaks about the 'Lord who quickens the dead', also of the 'World to come' which is usually seen as Heaven. This might be the case for some but, for most people, it is the next incarnation and the kind of life they will be born into. Kabbalists usually speak in metaphors about reincarnation but in *The Zohar*, the classic of its literature, there is a realistic description of how the soul which is about to reincarnate hovers above a love-making couple about to conceive the physical vehicle for the individual who will come into their lives.

As regards death, the opposite pole to birth, Kabbalah—like other traditions—talks of the separation of the soul from the body and how it hangs around for about a week. This is why there is the Jewish tradition of holding a series of services for seven days—even though the body might have been buried the day after death. The deceased individual, it is said, then spends some time (a year is a symbolic period) reviewing the life just passed, before moving on from a phase of purification or 'purgatory' to a stage appropriate to its level of development in the invisible worlds.

For most people, this means a return to the Treasure House of Souls, on the plane of the lower Earthly Paradise. This, it is said, closely resembles an ideal form of the physical world where they meet their deceased loved ones. It can mean family or a soul group of dear friends. Some of these relatives and companions may be at the point where they are about to depart, either to be reincarnated below again on Earth or rise to a higher level in the Heavenly upper Paradise where they will enter what are called the *Yeshivas* or Academies on High. These are the advanced Schools of the Soul and Spirit.

Bad people who have died are given the possibility of redemption, if they acknowledge the evil they have done, during the purgatorial period of reviewing the last life. If they are still in denial, they go to what is known traditionally as *Gehenna* or Hell. This, it is said, has seven levels, the lowest being quite unbearable so that nobody except the proud or stupid wishes to remain there. Such disembodied individuals are tormented by their own unconscious which is still operational as the psyche is still quite intact after death. Their suffering is symbolised, in many other cultures, in terms of intense and seemingly painful physical conditions, as Hell is close to the material dimension. The stories of ghosts, found worldwide, bears witness to this phenomenon. For example, violent souls sometimes take possession

Figure 90—BIRTH
The process of reincarnation begins with conception. The descending psyche is then attached to the embryo within the body of their future mother, selected by karma. In most cases the parents belong to the same soul group, social class and culture. More advanced individuals are usually born into a family appropriate for the development of that soul and themselves. In some cases a great spirit with a mission may be born into an ordinary family so as to be protected and matured until the moment to act comes. This can be seen in the birth chart which sets out the programme for a person. (Woodcut, 16th century.)

of criminals while the ghosts of alcoholics haunt taverns and imbibe through living drunkards who have glimpses of Hell in their stupors. This unpleasantness has its purpose, so as to wean them from descending further, to become what are known as the 'Living Dead'. This degenerate class of individuals can be seen in the evil addict, habitual criminals and political and religious tyrants who are responsible for the callous deaths of millions by war and persecution.

There is also the Kabbalistic concept of the *Dibbuk* or lost soul, still strongly attached to the physical realm. These deceased individuals cannot rise up, for some reason, from the Earth level of reality to begin the *post mortem* process that all who die must go through. It may be that they are too attached to sensual pleasures or do not wish to face what they have done in the phase of Purgatory. Some suicides belong to this zone of Limbo. They, it is said, often remain Earth-bound for the life span they were ordained to have. Sometimes these disembodied people seek to gain access to the living by seeking to enter a weakly defended psyche and take possession of their mind and body. This is often an attempt to reincarnate without having to face the assessment of the Afterlife. Possession by a deceased psyche is sometimes the reason for schizophrenia. A few psychiatrists have discreetly acknowledged that some mental patients are, indeed, a battleground between a dead and a living soul. Specialist clergy and occultists have methods to deal with such situations, if the host body and mind can participate in ejecting the dead intruder.

As can be seen, there is a vast array of human situations to be found in the lower two Worlds. So far we have dealt, briefly, with the first two journeys of being born, death and reincarnation. The third journey, as previously noted, is about coming back to aid this process. This operation is about the meaning of destiny which is quite different from fate. Fate is about one specific life; destiny is concerned with the string of these incarnations and their long-term significance as regards to two upper worlds and mankind's general evolution.

142

Figure 91—HISTORY
While nature has taken millions of years to evolve, humans have achieved much in ten millennia. However, humanity has to follow the same cosmic plan. The Stone Age corresponds to the mineral epoch, the agricultural revolution to that of vegetation while the animal phase is seen in the first empires. The fully human period began when the first ethical laws were drafted, of which the Ten Commandments is a classic example. Beyond this point, in this 16th century print, are the rungs of psychological and spiritual evolution symbolised by the angel and stars. At the top step is the contact with the lowest level of the Divine, represented by the Heavenly Jerusalem. (Ramon Lull's version of Jacob's Ladder.)

9. Evolution

In one of the early Kabbalistic accounts of visions of the upper worlds, a rabbinic mystic was shown a vast *Pargod* or Curtain that hangs down in front of the Throne of Heaven. Its design was made up of vegetable, animal and metal threads. This was a Time map of History. Most of the weave represented what the ancient Greeks called the mass of the common people, inasmuch as they lived very similar lives of toil. The animal threads were related to uncommon people, that is those whose lives were devoted to wealth, fame or power. In contrast, the silver threads were referred to those the Greek called heroines and heroes; that is, historic individuals of lesser destiny. The golden filaments represented those of greater destiny who served a higher sacred purpose.

The curtain was woven into a series of patterns. These symbolised different epochs — times of peace and war; calm and revolution; chaos and order. The configurations were made up of the threads that ran from the top of the curtain to the bottom and back again. In some areas a plain background predominated, signifying uneventful times; in others there were elaborate animal thread designs indicating, perhaps, a great empire. Here and there were beautiful knots of silver and gold threads, representing high points of civilisation. There were also jewels, indicating the presence of a school of the soul or spirit.

Each one of us is a thread in this metaphor. Some of us are embedded deep in the weave and others are right on the surface. The threads are, moreover, interwoven to produce a particular generation that might leave its mark or little trace, according to our collective karma. Kabbalists speak of different epochs in which we work out our individual destiny. One particular soul group might be concerned with exploration, another with invention and yet another with art, science or religion. One of life's aims is to know what the purpose of our particular thread is and how it fits into the pattern of the time we live in.

The first step to discover who we really are is to become aware of

144

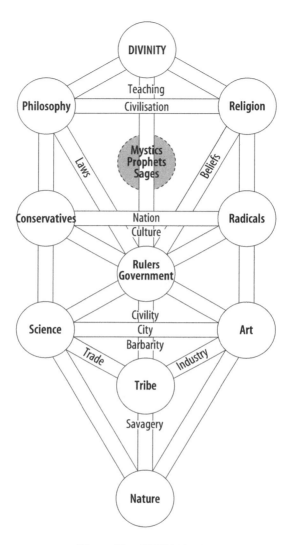

Figure 92—CIVILISATION
Here the various stages of development are set out. The anthropological term,
savagery, denotes the most primitive society. Barbarity is the phase when tribes
trade as well as make war. The rise of the city gave birth to a leisured class that
generated art and science. Out of cities arose nations and empires, governed by
a ruling animal level elite. However, civilisation could not occur until priests,
philosophers guided by mystics, created sacred and secular belief systems. While
influenced by local culture, their source was from the universal Teaching found
the world over. (Halevi.)

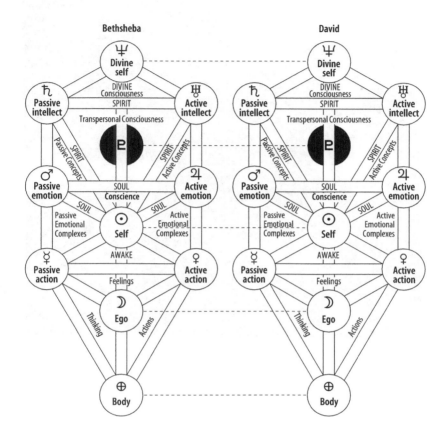

Figure 93—SOUL MATES
Here two individuals, a man and a woman, are drawn together because they have
certain things in common or resonate, according to Ascendant or body type, the
position of the Sun, Moon and planets in their birth charts. This is the story of
King David and the beautiful Bethsheba, the wife of another. According to some
Kabbalists, their encounter was a test of their integrity even though they were
soul mates. Such moral trials occur in the process of individual evolution. They
had to pay a price when the first son died. However, later the soul Solomon was
born to them. Even Solomon, though, succumbed to the temptations of sex,
wealth and power. (Halevi.)

Figure 94—CLUES
Traces of the Teaching are to be found everywhere. For example, the story of Cinderella is about the soul being confined to the kitchen by her stepmother and her ugly daughters who represent the ego and the body's instincts. Aladdin is another, with its four caves and the lamp which symbolises the four worlds and enlightenment. In Kabbalah there are many oblique references to hidden treasure in Jewish folklore, like the man who was told in a dream to go to a distant place where he would hear about the site of a great treasure trove. When he got there he was informed about a place that matched his own home. The Teaching was within his own heart. (The seeker following the footprints of Truth, Alchemical engraving.)

the fact that we are largely ruled by habit. Nearly all our thoughts, feelings and actions are determined by our family, social and cultural conditioning. While this is necessary for young souls, who have to learn how to conform to their society because they cannot survive on their own, more mature people need to know how to be individuals. Abraham, according to Biblical legend, disagreed with his father about idols and left Ur. Jacob, his grandson, was forced to leave home in order to develop the birthright that should have gone to Esau who was too unevolved to be worthy of and responsible for such a spiritual inheritance. This is a warning not to take one's potential destiny for granted. There is always someone who can fill that role, if needed.

King Saul is a classic example. His animal-level jealousy of young David and his consequent insanity reveal that he was not up to the task of being the Messiah of his time. Even David failed when he seduced Bethsheba and, indirectly, murdered her husband. However, he did recognise his misdemeanours and suffered in remorse and grief over their still-born child. Because of these and other flaws, David was not allowed to build the Temple. This is why the Bible has been so influential. It speaks of human beings as they are and the Law of Consequence and salvation in admission of wrong-doing. There is little sentiment about moral questions. The term, 'an eye for an eye' is not about revenge but karma, should conscience be ignored.

Many people on the early stages of the Path of Self-realisation go through what Saul, David and many other Biblical characters experienced. These failures indicate that we often learn more from our stupidity. However, separating ourselves out from life's hurly-burly is never recommended by Kabbalah, as life is the theatre and university of humanity. There is the story of a brilliant rabbinic student who neglected his studies for a year because he had fallen insanely in love with the village Venus. When he returned to his *Yeshiva*, broken-hearted and ashamed, he was severely rebuked by his rabbi. But as he was about to leave, having been accepted back into the school, the rabbi said with a flicker of a smile, 'Indeed, she was very beautiful'. A great Master who had been through the crisis himself understood the deviation. A teacher without such an experience could not have had such compassion. Here is Justice and Mercy in action.

Kabbalah learns from everyday events as well as from books and spiritual practice. 'One can even learn about being alert from a thief who is ever watchful for an opportunity', observed one rabbi. He was referring to what is called the *Gadlut*—elated mindfulness of being

Figure 95—TIMING

In the course of a nation or individual's life, there are times when nothing can be done and others when many things are possible. This is due to a combination of terrestrial and celestial conditions. For example, if a country suffers from drought, civilisation cannot arise. Likewise, an individual has to be relatively balanced to exploit their full potential. Both situations are partially contingent upon the positions of the heavenly bodies, for even nations have birth charts. England, for instance, came into being at noon on 25th December 1066 when William the Conqueror was crowned. As an entity, it is clearly Capricornian with its old traditions, class system and a gift for practical organisation. (Astrological engraving, 17th century.)

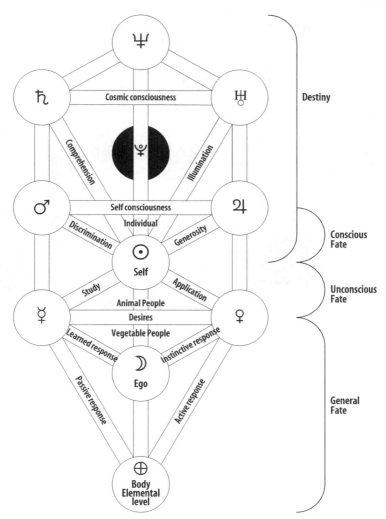

Figure 96—CHOICE
Individuals and nations can choose to make the most of their moments of opportunity or miss them. Those that decline the chance remain at the level they have achieved. This may be at the vegetable or animal stages for some people and nations. However, individuals and countries can, at their peak, or even a low point, become instruments of destiny. Britain, when alone in 1940, led by Churchill staved off the destruction of Western civilisation. In this Tree, the levels are all set out but they are subject to the Solar, Lunar and planetary state of the sefirot. Only those who are highly evolved are above the influence of the stars. (Halevi.)

Figure 97—DESTINY
Napoleon was a remarkable individual. His birth chart with Sun in Leo, Moon in Capricorn and Libra on the Ascendant indicated that he would be a charismatic leader. He brought the French Revolution under control and he set up a system of law that recognised all citizens as equal. However, Napoleon succumbed to the Lucific temptation of power and marred his destiny on becoming the emperor of a vast French empire. The result was that from being admired, he became the most feared man in Europe. He died in disgrace on a remote island. (Napoleon Emancipating Jews, 19th century.)

conscious of being conscious. Only in this state can one begin to climb the Holy Mountain. The tradition also says it is vital to have an experienced guide who knows the Path and the pitfalls. This requires the seeker of Truth to find someone who at least knows about the foothills of Heaven. A brilliant but naïve scholar, or holy fool, is not a real help. Better a worldly-wise business person for a Kabbalistic tutor, as was often the case, as not a few great rabbis were also master traders.

There is the story of a great merchant who had everything but life was empty. He wanted to be of use to his community but it rejected him. He asked his rabbi what was wrong. The rabbi said, 'Go to the window and tell me what you see'. The man looked out onto the village street and saw old friends of his youth who now deliberately ignored him. This hurt him deeply. Then the rabbi said, 'Look in the mirror by the window; what do you see?' The merchant turned and said, 'Just myself'. The rabbi then asked, 'What is the difference between the window and the mirror?' The man thought for a moment and replied, 'The silver on the back of the mirror.' Silver, or *kesef* in Hebrew, also means money. He got the point. From that day on he opened up his mansion to all, invited the needy in and gave much to charity. From that time on, he became a respected and beloved member of his community and, in time, a discreet teacher of Kabbalah.

The lesson here is that an animal man who has achieved his aim can recognise that it is time to move on and be trained to become a teacher. Some people believe they can develop alone because they possess a little spiritual knowledge. This can be a destructive delusion. These proud and often arrogant individuals usually believe themselves to be very superior and have no need for a tutor. When they do meet a master they either fail to recognise them or, if they do sense some wisdom, ignore or even denigrate someone who could further their progress. This phenomenon is called a Lucific temptation. The genuine seeker will know and acknowledge anyone further on and seek to learn all they can from them, be it but an encounter of an hour or over a lifetime.

One prerequisite for the 'Work', as it is sometimes called, is information. This is gleaned mostly from books or conversations with well-informed people. The texts may be from ancient or medieval sources or popular lectures on Kabbalah that can either make things clear or more of a muddle. Here discrimination is vital. Then there are what are called 'preparatory schools' that run courses on Kabbalah.

Figure 98—TEACHER

It is the task of an instructor of the soul to guide a pupil to the Path and set them up on it by imparting higher knowledge and being a moral example. This is the function of a genuine rabbi or priest. Many of the clergy may appear to be learned but are really only interested in prestige. The Bible and history are full of such examples. Take the corrupt sons of Eli, the High Priest, and the decadent Borgia Pope Alexander VI. In this illustration a certain Rabbi Nathan brings a flash of enlightenment to a student who claimed it was like the Sun coming out at night. Unfortunately, his words were taken literally so that when there was a fire in the Jewish quarter the rabbi got the blame. Being an esoteric teacher has its hazards which is why most are very discreet. (Rabbi enlightening students, 19th century.)

These can be genuine, fake or a mixture. In one sense it does not matter where one learns about the Tradition as long as it opens up possibilities. What is important is that one learns that Kabbalah is a working method, discipline and route to psychological and spiritual development.

Astrology and magic are as ancient as Kabbalah. Many people hear about Kabbalah—or Cabala, as the Occult line calls it—by encountering those two approaches. Astrology is interesting and useful because it is a working system concerned with the soul, fate and destiny. Magic is more eclectic, that is, made up of bits and pieces of esoteric concepts and practices that can be a coherent discipline that gives access to the invisible realms. However, one must be sure the Teacher is a White and High magician and not one seeking Occult power, as this leads to delusion and sometimes destruction when forces become out of control.

It is said that the moment a soul or psyche becomes incarnate, its fluidic nature is crystallised into a particular form, according to the celestial situation. The pattern set out in the birth chart indicates, from the viewpoint of Kabbalistic astrologers, the karma the person is bringing in. This manifests in their character for this incarnation and what, in terms of fate, lies ahead. According to Kabbalah, just as the soul is about to be born, it is shown what people and events it will encounter. This vision is soon forgotten as bodily needs dominate the mind and the ego becomes increasingly conditioned. Later in life, if the person chooses to develop, they may begin to recognise, among friends and family, members of their soul group and what their destiny is. Kabbalistic astrology is very different from that found in the media and even classical astrology. It is concerned not only with the psychology of an individual as defined in the birth chart but also the various levels within it.

Most people live off their Moon sign. This means they never rise above their cultural conditioning. The Kabbalistic and the esoteric astrologer endeavour to make full use of the insights gained from studying their own horoscopes and those of others, so as to take advantage of the cosmic weather that governs not only world trade and politics but when personal opportunities open or when no action should be taken. For example, when the planet Saturn is in a particular position in a person's birth chart nothing seems to happen, whereas when Jupiter is there anything seems to bloom or explode. These phenomena have been observed over several millennia and statistically are as reliable as terrestrial weather, inasmuch as a particular trend can be taken into account as regards fate.

This is an example of an esoteric discipline being applied as an auxiliary working method. Many medieval Jewish poets and philosophers used astrology as an added tool, not only to understand the psyche, fate and Providence but also to learn about the rhythms and patterns of the Heavens at both the celestial and spiritual levels. The hallmark of any great master is that they are prepared to recognise the Truth in whatever form it may appear. This does not mean that one loses sight of one's own tradition but that such exchanges have deepened, over the centuries, the comprehension of the Teaching in its all-encompassing reality.

Perhaps the most crucial thing at this point of development, where the ordinary world seems to offer nothing real in the 'passing show', is to be able to find a real Teacher. He or she, as noted, might be a great sage or saint but they are more likely to be someone one meets in everyday life. However, they will have a certain inner light, calm or knowledge not found in the ordinary world. It may take a long time to find such a Kabbalistic tutor. There are many who claim to be masters but they are often inflated egos. The genuine master's character is usually modest, despite their rank. The search operation requires great attention as one can waste much time and even money on false trails that can lead one away from the Path. In some cases, a bad experience with a so-called school of the soul can put one off for this lifetime. Always check the integrity of those who teach. Do they practise what they teach? Are their students closed or open-minded and do they relate and operate well in the workaday world?

10. Teachers

It is said that when the student is ready, the Teacher appears. The reason for this is that the as yet unawakened individual does not notice anyone beyond their own psychological or spiritual level. They only see the obvious. A great prophet, in contrast, sees through the surface and beyond. However, a teacher need not be more than very sensitive, intelligent or psychic for they have only to be able to assess the capacity of a potential student and how to help them develop it. A master, however, will perceive the level of their soul and possible destiny. That is, in Kabbalistic terms, for what an individual was 'Called forth for, created, formed and made'.

In the Bible there are what are called the greater and lesser prophets. The greater could foresee coming historical events because they understood the laws of cause and effect and could identify the omens. They were able to do this while in a state of cosmic consciousness, as well as being fully aware of the present. Lesser prophets see in unfocused flashes and do not understand what they are seeing. The priests in the Tabernacle and Temple had an oracular device, the *Urim and Thummin* that, like the Chinese *I Ching*, gave symbolic answers that had to be interpreted. Kabbalists have various techniques, such as Bibliomancy, but these have to be used intelligently.

Most Kabbalistic tutors rely on a sound training in theory, practice and long experience. While some teachers have a natural talent for 'insight', others have to work for it. In time, as individuals develop their higher 'centres', the ability to intuit becomes active. These faculties relate to the Hindu chakras and parallel the sefirot in the body and the psyche. Prophets draw upon the higher sefirot of knowledge, understanding and wisdom that give rise to direct mystical experience, deep comprehension and profound inspiration. Everyone, it is said, has at least one moment in their lives in which these capacities are operational.

A good tutor should have a thorough grounding in the Tradition's psychological and spiritual disciplines. They must have passed tests

Figure 99—ENLIGHTENMENT
When Moses came down from Mount Sinai, his face was so radiant that the Israelites could not bear to look at it. In lesser mortals the radiance is not so bright but it is the hallmark of much interior work and the result of intense study and practice over a long period. A moment of Divine Grace can have a similar effect but the radiance fades if not sustained by effort. Some people at the start of their spiritual development want a teacher of Moses' calibre. However, they usually have to be content with an instructor who is just ahead of them in evolution. This is the first test of their commitment. (Bank's Bible, 19th century.)

Figure 100—ELIJAH

He is an Earthly manifestation of Enoch who can appear anywhere and at any time in history. He comes to teach and protect anyone worthy but does not suffer fools gladly. A rabbi asked Elijah if he could go with him on his current mission. The reply was yes, on condition no questions were asked. When crossing a river, Elijah bored a hole in a ferry boat. Later, after staying with a hospitable farming family, he pointed at their prize bull which dropped dead. The rabbi, unable to accept such seemingly malicious acts, asked why. The reply was that the hole meant that the ferry could not be used by bandits waiting to steal it and that he had redirected the Angel of Death to kill the bull, not the farmer's newborn son. The rabbi was then sent home, having learned his lesson. (Elijah restoring life to a dead child, Doré's *Bible Illustrations*, 19th century.)

158

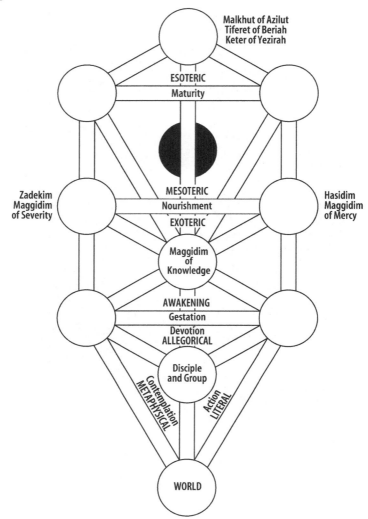

Figure 101—MAGGIDIM
This term is used for Kabbalistic teachers who are both in the flesh and discarnate.
The lower levels are those who teach the ways of Action, Devotion and
Contemplation. The upper maggidim, who nourish the soul, work on the aspects
of discipline and tolerance while the highest order instruct those who are fully
on the Path of the Spirit. The invisible tutors take charge of people on Earth if
there is no one of the right calibre available in that time and place. Generally
they tutor those of the same soul group. This guarantees that there is continuity
in the Teaching over the generations. (Halevi.)

regarding their integrity and not be seduced by the powers they acquire. They have always to be alert and well-informed about a student's situation. More importantly, they must know their own strengths and weaknesses and their psyche's shadow side. Most of all, they should have a sense of proportion and a very good sense of humour. Without these last two, the rest can be quite dangerous. Many a would-be master has destroyed their possibilities by taking themselves too seriously.

There are, in general, three types of teachers. These relate to the Ways of Action, Devotion and Contemplation. They arise often according to physical build and psychological disposition of a tutor. For example, those who tend towards the chubby are usually 'feelers' while the muscular is invariably a practical person. Those of slender, nervous physique are inclined to be 'thinkers'. There is also the astrological factor. An Aries tutor will set challenges for their students whereas a Capricorn will prefer to ponder ideas; while a Piscean would use meditation to teach. Students, moreover, tend to be drawn to tutors of a similar element, like Earth to Earth being attracted by a no-nonsense approach, in contrast to Air signs that love to discuss concepts.

An advanced teacher, of whatever Line, is someone who has established a connection with what are called, in Kabbalah, the *Maggidim*. These are discarnate teachers of a higher order who watch over and instruct those on Earth, in the front line of human development. There is the story of the students of an eminent rabbi who saw, as they passed by his study window, their teacher conversing with a wise-looking old man. However, when they entered the rabbi's room, the old gentleman had gone. But where and how, the students wondered, as there was no other door out of the study? One was told years later, when he could understand, that it was Elijah whom they saw talking to the master.

Such remarkable teachers as this are usually, moreover, protected by Providence, that is, the Heavenly organisation responsible for taking care of such people. Take the case of the great mystic on a long journey. He could not find anyone in an extremely unfriendly village to give him a bed for the night. Because of this, he had to sleep in the forest. In the morning, he discovered that the village had been attacked by marauders who killed everyone. Clearly he was not meant to be part of this evil village's karma. In another legend, a famous old rabbi was being hunted down by the Roman authorities for his anti-government

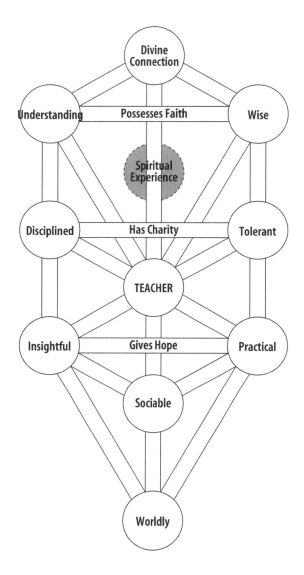

Figure 102—MASTER
By this is meant someone who has direct, conscious access to the Higher Worlds and not just bookish knowledge. The qualities of such a person are here set out on the Tree. Foremost, they must be balanced and have experience of the ordinary world. Some of the greatest masters have not been scholars or priests. Indeed, they can be either conservative or radical, rich or poor. There is no fixed rôle. Their hallmark is a love of people, the Truth and God. (Halevi.)

Figure 103—FABLES
Often after the death of a great teacher, stories of their wisdom and achievements are embroidered beyond recognition. Rabbi Lowe of Prague was an enlightened, open minded scholar. During the Renaissance alchemy, astrology and magic were of great interest. He was acquainted with these subjects. Because of this, he was seen by some as a great magician who created a Golem, a living humanoid made of clay, to protect the Jews. This fable was, in fact, about another rabbi but Rabbi Lowe has been seen ever since as the original Dr Frankenstein. Lesson: do not believe everything said about Kabbalah. (Rabbi Lowe statue, Prague.)

Figure 104—SEER

Nostradamus came from a Jewish converso family. He was a physician, astrologer, Kabbalist and prophet. Besides medical prognostication, he could peer into the future and, together with a knowledge of historic patterns, foresee key events, such as the English Civil War, the Great Fire of London and the French revolution. In fear of the Inquisition he clothed his predictions in obscure verse that only revealed themselves when they occurred. Needless to say, there were inaccuracies, such as calling Hitler 'Hister'. However, weather and economic forecasts are not much better. Some Kabbalists have the gift but it must be used with great care. (Engraving, 17th century.)

views. He was traced by officials to a small inn. However, when they burst into his room they were surprised to find him in the company of a beautiful courtesan. Now, while the rabbi was known to be a political dissident, his reputation for moral integrity was without question. The officials concluded they had obviously tracked down the wrong person. The moment they left, the courtesan vanished into thin air. It is said that she was a manifestation of Enoch, the Master of time, space and any form he could take, in protecting one of the most important teachers on Earth in that period.

One may smile at such charming and quaint tales but many people on the spiritual Path have experienced such extraordinary synchronicities in dangerous situations; indeed, miraculous interventions that have saved them from disaster. Who has not had a sense, at crucial points in their life, of the strong, invisible presence of someone who indicates that a dubious action or decision should not be taken. Socrates spoke of his 'daemon' or invisible mentor. Sometimes it is a deceased relative. For others it might be a long-dead tutor, like the Kabbalist who discovered that his invisible guide was an 11th century poet and philosopher. This Maggid's name and place of birth were confirmed by a forgotten book being drawn to the Kabbalist's attention and a vivid image of a Spanish harbour as seen from a Moorish fortress. This place of birth was confirmed by the student, standing on the wall of the Malaga *Alcazaba* and seeing the identical view of the modernised harbour. A bronze statue of Ibn Gabirol now stands at the foot of the citadel.

At the beginning of their Second Journey, people need to know about the basic theory and practice of a tradition. In Kabbalah, the conventional way is through a rabbinic college. But this way is not open to all. Moreover many seekers, both Jewish and otherwise, want to follow the more secular line as they are well educated within a broader Western culture that takes into account modern science, psychology and a wide field of travel and everyday experience. Therefore Providence, ever ready to meet the needs of a time and place, has various kinds of Kabbalists posted in various parts of the world. The Kabbalah, contrary to popular belief, is not exclusive. Indeed, the destiny of the Jewish people is to be 'A Light unto Nations'. The many different ethnic strains seen in modern Judaism bear witness to the number of conversions over the centuries. As quoted, there is no religion higher than Truth and Kabbalah is a Spiritual tradition that should be open to all who seek the Holy One.

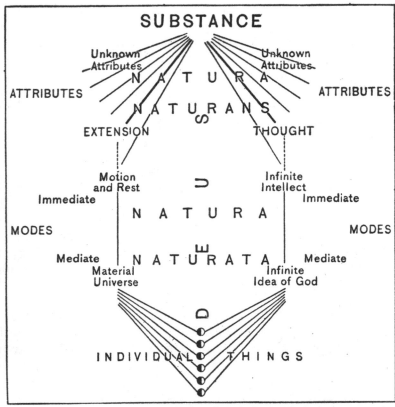

Diagram Illustrating Spinoza's Metaphysical System.

Figure 105—SPINOZA

This Jewish philosopher was brought up in the orthodox tradition and studied Kabbalah. However, he was particularly fascinated by the 17th century European preoccupation with pure reason to explain the nature of the universe, its purpose and God. As can be seen from this diagram, there is a strong correspondence with the Sefirotic Tree. Because of a seemingly cold intellectual approach, he was regarded by Amsterdam's rabbis as a heretic. He continued his work, teaching a group from the university town of Leyden. Ironically, his effort to update Kabbalah followed in the footsteps of such medieval metaphysicians as Ibn Gabirol of Malaga and Azriel of Gerona. The value of his effort was recognised later when the Age of Reason established the modern philosophical method. (Jewish Encyclopaedia.)

Figure 106—INSPIRATION
Solomon ibn Gabirol lived in Spain in the 11th century. He wrote sacred hymns,
love poems, wise sayings and a philosophical thesis on Existence as well as a
poetic version of Jacob's Ladder. He was familiar with royal court life and
Bohemian style culture of the great Moorish period, as well as his own Jewish
heritage. As a person he criticised himself harshly as being ugly and very
conceited because of his great talent. Despite this, his spirit has been an
inspiration to many Kabbalists including this author, seen standing by his statue
in Malaga in Spain. (Photograph Jon Cooper Taylor, 21st century.)

To find one's Teacher means to be actively aware. One may meet or miss them on a journey, at a party or even at work. If such a person considers you a possible candidate, they may drop hints that only those who are conscious of what is being said will recognise. These might come in the form of an indirect question or a subtle implication. If one is sensitive, one may note that such a person emits a kind of light or has a non-physical pleasant aroma about them. They can appear to be quite ordinary but have a presence or a penetrating gaze that is very different from a sharp glance. They often have a kind of grace and a quality of beauty, even though they may not be conventionally good-looking or quite old. This is the hallmark of a refined and advanced soul. Be watchful.

Likewise, one may encounter a school of the soul in a great city or the country. It may not advertise or even be known but its students will have a certain demeanour of discretion, certainty or centredness that marks them out. Their social or professional status is irrelevant in the Kabbalistic tradition. Some of the greatest practitioners have lived very modest lives while others have served as advisors in royal courts. One rabbi discovered that his teacher was a street market trader. Moreover, not all are scholars and some even have only a little Hebrew. Books are helpful but not vital as it is only direct experience that can be regarded as first-hand. The invisible but sometimes quite audible Maggidim will reveal things that are not recorded in any writings. This was the original definition of the Oral Tradition.

11. Schools

Every culture has some sort of school of the soul. It might take place in a forest glade, a circle of stone or a huge Temple. In Kabbalah it could be the back room of the synagogue, the salon of a private house or even out in the open, as described in *The Zohar*. The point is that there has to be a place to meet. This is the Malkhut of the Tree of any school. Like any organism or organisation, a school is based on the sefirotic model, otherwise it will not function as a complete entity. It may be unconsciously arrived at by conforming to what works or carefully and deliberately designed, as it was in the case of the Temple in Jerusalem.

The next element, at Yesod or the Foundation, is that of the students. These may be in a formal situation, as in the rabbinic Yeshiva, or an informal arrangement in someone's home. Schools may manifest in an annual congress, a weekly gathering or an everyday meeting. Some schools may come into being for a short period, others for just a teacher's lifetime or be in existence for several centuries. Likewise, they may consist of a local handful of committed individuals or a large ongoing stream of people passing through an organised system of training. Unlike the usual academic or religious establishments, a school of the soul may have no fixed outer form. Moreover, it may be radical or conservative by nature, depending upon the need of the time and place, be it in a remote village or at the centre of a great civilisation.

One example of an unconventional school was the medieval rabbi who had his wife teach basics to newcomers. This was discreetly done, as it did not conform with the current culture. This occurred because she had the knowledge and skill to teach and was better at introducing the system to newcomers. Contrary to common belief, as there were women Judges in the Bible so there have been female mystics. The wife of the great Rabbi Akiba, according to legend, had greater foresight than he while the wife of Rabbi Meir, it is said, was wiser than her husband when it came to dealing with reality. In Jewish legend Miriam, Moses' sister had, as noted, a well that moved with

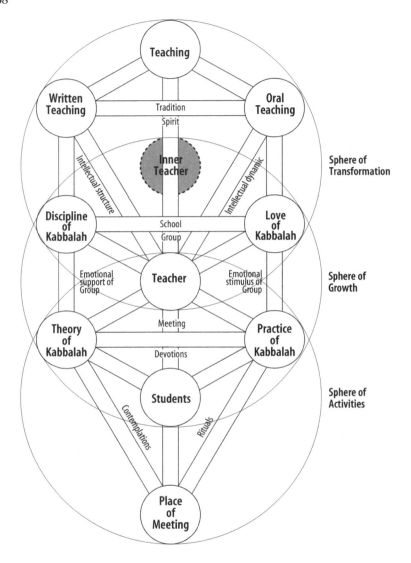

Figure 107—SCHOOL OF THE SOUL
Such an organisation has to have all the functions and levels set out in this Tree.
It is not enough, moreover, just to study Kabbalah and put into practice its various
methods. There has to be a serious commitment to the school and its aim; in this
case, the development of both its students and teachers. The side triads indicate
what is needed while the central column defines the seven levels of the school
with the Spirit of its founder hovering at Daat, the place of Knowledge. (Halevi.)

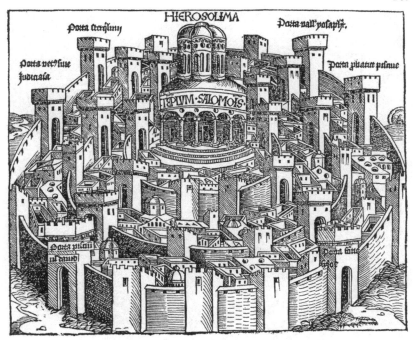

Figure 108—SCHOOLS

In ancient Jerusalem there were many schools in and around the Temple. Each had its own approach. Some were esoteric and others more academic. There were also the ultra-orthodox and unconventional schools. This medieval Christian woodcut conveys the impression of concentration that is still present in the city. Then, as now, schools of every level are to be found, of different traditions' lines. The Kabbalists generally kept a low profile and were only found by those who knew what to look for. (Medieval Jerusalem, woodcut.)

Figure 109—MEETING
This can be an informal affair or a ritualistic operation. Here it is at a Passover supper where the inner meaning of the Exodus is acted out and discussed. It is here that initiations take place but not in a conventional way. They occur when a student is alert to, perhaps, a loaded remark by the rabbi that makes him awake. Then a new understanding and inner process begins that takes the student onto the next rung of Jacob's Ladder. Such silent events are usually only observed by the master at the end of the table. (Passover Haggadah, 17th century.)

the Israelites through the desert from which people could drink. This is a way of saying she had a psychic capacity, this being symbolised by water, the element of the realm of Formation. Because Miriam possessed psychological insight, people came to her for advice. Unfortunately at one point she believed she was Moses' equal. This occurs when the personal is mistaken for the transpersonal of the Spirit. This was a Lilith temptation for which she was severely chastised, as there was more at stake than her inflated ego. Later, as said, Moses suffered from an inflated moment of Self which was a warning to every great teacher to be mindful of their limits.

When a seeker makes contact with a real school of the soul, they are usually seen by a senior member. If they are regarded as a suitable member, a situation is sometimes set up to find out just how reliable or committed the person might be. It could be, for example, to be told to make contact with someone at an awkward time or difficult place. True seekers invariably turn up on the dot whereas those with just a passing interest in the esoteric might ignore or even forget about the appointment. Schools of the soul have not got time for people who are not serious.

There are different levels of school within the ways of Action, Devotion and Contemplation. Some are preparatory groups. These introduce people to the theory and practice of that particular line. A course might take a year with each individual tested to see how involved they are in the Work. They might be asked to do certain mundane duties, such as cleaning, buying food or taking notes. These operations get rid of those whose enthusiasm soon fades. The story of Jacob having to work many years to make Rachel his wife is symbolic of this. Often the most seemingly keen quickly drop out, usually to go to another school and then another, all their lives, always backing off when real effort is required. These are defined as occult dilettantes who never commit themselves to genuine development.

Once it is seen that an individual is truly committed to the Path, they are admitted to the main body of a school. This may take the form of a ceremony or be a simple welcome, depending on the custom of that line. Originally, the Bar Mitzvah served this purpose. It signified that a boy was now to be considered as an adult. It was symbolic of no longer being one of the as-yet unawakened Children of Israel but an evolving member of the House of Israel.

Here there has to be a word of warning. There are Schools of the Soul and teachers that are not what they appear. For example, a school

Figure 110—PLACE
Meetings have not always been in the synagogue. They can occur in the rabbi's home where, it is said, women joined in, contrary to custom. It has been known for the rabbi's wife to lead a group. This was done very discreetly. Sometimes meetings took place in the house of a rich merchant or a poor scholar's home. Accordingly, people might meet in the palace of a Jewish official, as seen here. This place in Toledo belonged to a minister of finance. Such high-positioned individuals would support masters like Ibn Gabirol. In Moorish times, there would be discussions between the mystics of all three religions. The Sufis and Kabbalists have much in common. (Toledo, medieval house.)

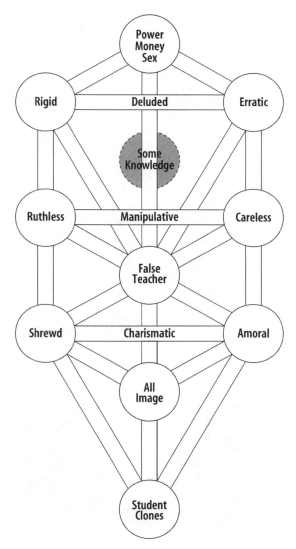

Figure 111—DARK TEACHER
Knowledge is power and not a few teachers have been tempted to use esoteric principles to exploit the gullibility of others. By this is meant that students are given a certain amount of information and some practices that work which convinces them that their teacher is a great master, even though they never quite let them in on the so-called 'secrets'. Unfortunately, those close to such a leader sometimes collude in the operation to gain status, in the hope of inheriting the mantle of the false master. (Halevi.)

Figure 112—SPREAD OF KABBALAH
The Jews were to be found throughout Europe, the Middle and Far East and even
China and possibly Japan. Many later settled in the Americas. A large number
moved to the Netherlands where Kabbalah was studied by Protestants who read
the Old Testament according to new understanding. There were discreet lectures
on Kabbalah in England and it had an influence upon Freemasonry. The founder
of the Theosophical Society, Madam Blavatsky, likewise drew upon the Kabbalah,
as did the magical order of the Golden Dawn. (Masonic Theory Board with
Solomon's pillars, Jacob's Ladder and the old Hebrew Name of God.)

may be no more than a shell of what was once a living tradition. Over time it had, perhaps, become run down having spent its force but still believes it has a purpose. In another case it might be a school that has been taken over by people more interested in power or the money it can generate, its 'teacher' living well off followers who believe he or she possesses real knowledge. The image of such organisations is usually maintained by someone who has some esoteric theory or practices but has no concept of what the Work is really about. An applicant to any school must test those who invite them in and closely observe their leader to make sure they are genuine. One of the signs to note is a certain arrogance and excessive discipline that holds its members in total obedience to a ruling elite. These are usually senior members of the school who have either fallen under the spell of a 'Dark Teacher' or who collude with him or her because it gives them a personal status they could not possibly attain in the outside world. One sign is to make everyone conform. Indeed, a symptom that a school is dying or dead is that the members are uniform in dress, in manners and ideas or based upon the personality cult of the leader. In some cases the clothes they wear belong to another epoch, as do their attitudes. This cuts them off from general evolution that has moved on. They often claim only they have the true teaching and are hostile to other schools.

In a living school there is usually an openness, even though there may be great discipline. This is because of a discernment and tolerance of others whose temperament and approach might be different. Another sign is that the leader speaks to everyone with equal attention and in their terms. In the everyday world, this is called the 'common touch;' that is, the ability to relate to every type of person. While a teacher may hold the Tiferet position on the Tree of the school, they must be able to communicate with every student. This means be practical, imaginative and intellectual as well as being down to Earth, psychological and a mystic. This is the hallmark of a Master Teacher.

The triad of Tiferet, Hod and Nezah is concerned with meetings and initiations. These again might be formal but the real process of initiation takes place within each person as they begin the next phase of development. It can sometimes occur during a meeting, stimulated by a remark by the teacher, during a ceremony, while practising one's profession or even at home. It can also happen while on an inner journey to the celestial Jerusalem. This is a Kabbalistic exercise in which, through a guided meditation, one might visit the Academy on

(Above) Figure 113—TODAY
Since the 1960s, Kabbalah has come into the public domain through the New Age movement. This was because of the lack of spirituality in organised religions. People in search of the truth about the purpose of Existence travelled far and wide to find answers. For some, Kabbalah had the esoteric approach that appealed to them. Thus many study groups arose. The line illustrated here followed the medieval Spanish tradition of mystical philosophy, as applied to modern psychology, contemplation and meditation. (A meeting place in 20th century London.)

(Right) Figure 114—ASCENT
To climb the Ladder of Self-realisation means to pass through many levels. First there is the ability to manage ordinary life skilfully; then ascend the seven levels of the psyche, before entering the Great Spiritual Mysteries of the seven Halls of Heaven. Here the 'Watchers' check anyone who seeks to go beyond their capacity. Not a few aspirants believe that once they experience a flash of cosmic consciousness they have achieved their goal. To encounter the Divine Realm requires many qualities, such as commitment, courage and integrity, and to be able to overcome the temptations while going up the Ladder. (Halevi.)

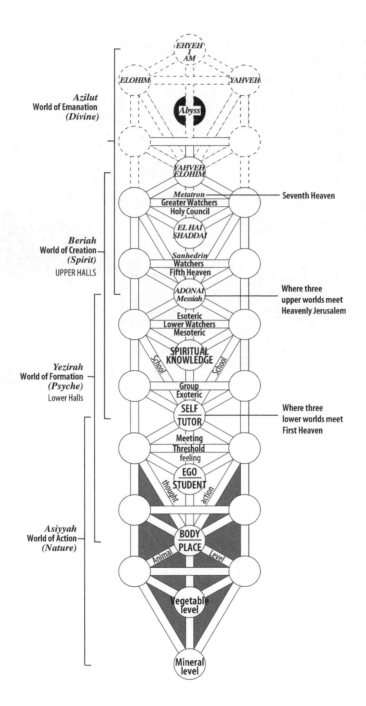

Figure 115—SAFED

After the expulsion from Spain in 1492, many Kabbalists migrated to the Galilean hill town of Safed because it resembled, in many ways, a Spanish environment. Here a number of schools were set up because it was close to the grave of Rabbi Simeon ben Yochai, the supposed author of The Zohar. The group that used to meet in the chamber shown here was led by an eminent rabbi, Joseph Karo, who would go into a semi-trance and speak with wisdom beyond his normal capacity. In other schools there would be detailed discussions about the sefirot or a Kabbalistic version of a traditional ritual. (Rabbi Karo's synagogue, 16th century.)

High. Through an act of conscious imagination, it is possible to see one's own Maggid. Such a moment of vision and transformation can change the outlook of a lifetime into a revelation about one's fate or destiny.

The triad of Tiferet, Gevurah and Hesed is that of that particular school, the equivalent to the triad of the soul in the individual psyche. This usually takes its character from the school's founder. They may have long passed on but their legacy continues until it is no longer relevant to a new period. Often such advanced people will choose to be reborn to renovate the school or start another that has a new mission. An example of this was the Baal Shem Tov who had to meet and deal with a specific circumstance. He may well have been a member of the Essene movement in ancient Palestine which had similar values to his 18th century Hassidic school.

It is said that after their death, the spirit of the teacher sometimes hovers in the non-sefirah of Daat of a school. Their task is to oversee its progress to make sure it enters into the great Tiferet-Hokhmah-Binah triad so that it becomes part of a mainstream spiritual tradition, such as Kabbalah. The left side triad of philosophy, law and science or the structural elements, together with the right side dynamic factors of religion, art and literature, are the basis of civilisation. At the centre of this complex is Daat, the esoteric factor. In Islam the Sufis hold this position while in ancient China the Taoists represented the mystical dimension of the empire. Without this presence and influence, there would be no evolution.

In the topmost triad is the Torah or essential Teaching. This is universal. As one of the most influential but largely unknown spiritual masters of the ancient Western world, the Teaching of Plotinus of Alexandria has underpinned the inspirational aspect of the Christian, Islamic and Jewish mysticism. Such pure knowledge is to be recognised by Native American, African and Asian Shamans, as well as within the sophisticated or subtle systems of India, China and Japan. For example, in the Shinto tradition the altar has three pillars, symbols for the four worlds and a dark mirror hung in the centre that corresponds to the black hole of Daat. It is only the outer form that is different.

The importance of Kabbalah is that it is part of the Judeo-Christian-Hellenic tradition that underlies the history of Western spirituality. This was, as noted, recognised in the Renaissance by the European intelligentsia. Indeed, Kabbalah made no small contribution to the

Figure 116—ASHKENAZIM
This is a term used to define the Northern and Eastern European Yiddish-speaking
Jews from the Ladino speaking Sefardim of southern Europe and the Middle
East. As a culture they were not philosophically minded but more inclined to
ritual, prayers and legal matters. However, they did take on the Lurianic version
of Kabbalah. In synagogues like the one shown here, Kabbalah would be studied
at night, after a session on the rabbinic commentaries. In the more primitive
conditions of old Russia they were strongly influenced by folklore and the more
mythical traditions of Kabbalah. (Russian synagogue, *Jewish Encyclopaedia*,
20th century.)

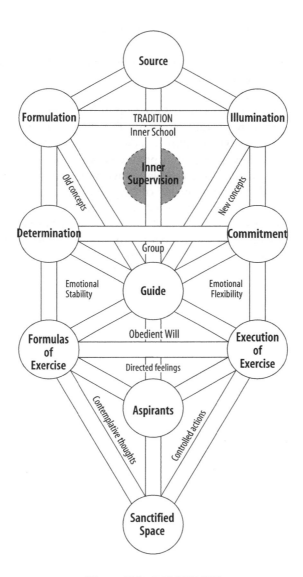

Figure 117—DISCIPLINE
Here the elements of the Kabbalistic path are set out. It is vital, for example, for the aspirant to be stable emotionally. Without this, they will falter when things become difficult. This sometimes occurs when major psychological changes happen. This is because a Kabbalist must cast aside many old patterns resulting from cultural conditioning. This Tree gives much guidance upon climbing the Holy Mountain. (Halevi.)

various schools of the soul as the Alchemists, Freemasons and the Golden Dawn. The Alchemists invented a complex, technical language which only the initiated could understand. Their texts and practices talked about making gold out of lead. This was a symbol about transforming the grosser parts of a human being into a more refined spiritual vehicle. It was based upon Kabbalistic principles, as was Freemasonry that used Solomon's Temple as a model.

At the present time, Kabbalah is undergoing a reincarnation, not out of ancient or medieval texts and practices but contemporary science and psychology which is the equivalent to the language of symbolism of the Bible and the metaphysics of the Middle Ages but in modern terms. There was tremendous resistance to philosophy in the Middle Ages with the books being burnt and people declared heretics for introducing a seemingly radical new form. The same resistance by the ultra-traditionalists is occurring in this 21st century but no one can stop evolution if it is meant to happen. There is nothing higher than Truth.

12. Theory

In Kabbalah, the most immediate and important area of study and practice is oneself. Without knowledge of human nature, which is the image of the Divine, there can be no wisdom or understanding, indeed any development. The two lowest Trees of Jacob's Ladder, that is, of the body and the psyche, are the two most accessible. When the anatomy of the physical organism is put on the Tree, the whole of the organic evolution can be seen. There are, for example, the seven levels of Nature. At Malkhut are the mineral, metal and elemental dimensions. Above, at Yesod, are the lower plants; then come the higher plants. These are followed by plant-animals; over them are seen the invertebrates, above which come the higher animals. At the top is humanity which incorporates all below. As regards the individual body, the four worlds are seen in miniature in the mechanical, chemical, electronic and conscious levels. These manifest in the various systems as seen in Figure 121.

This schematic vehicle is in the potential of the fertilised egg of the mother. However, according to Kabbalah, the body's configuration already exists in the realm of Formation. Called the *zelem* or shadow it is gradually filled out as the individual grows physically from infancy to adulthood. The zelem carries the psychological character over from the last and previous other lives. This accounts for the difference between siblings, even though they have the same family and ethnic genes. The embryonic body is connected with the psyche at the moment of conception and is fused with it at the moment of birth.

Some people can remember their birth and even what occurred prior to it. This can be recalling departing from old friends in the higher worlds or having a flash forward insight onto their fate. This, as noted, is partly determined by the state of the cosmos which holds the overall Divine Plan of evolution at the universal and individual levels. A birth chart is not about where the physical celestial bodies are in the sky but the astrological principles that govern life on Earth. For example, there can be no summer and all its activities without the Sun being in

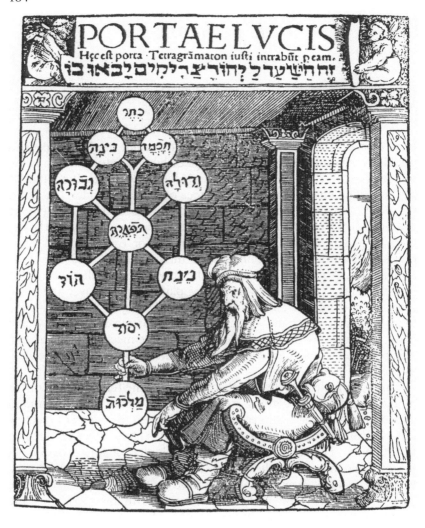

Figure 118—KNOWLEDGE
Only by getting to know the Sefirotic Tree thoroughly can a Kabbalist ascend safely. This is the key and map to the Way. Here, for example, is an incomplete version. Without all the paths and triads, nothing can happen as the process is incomplete. Many people have studied distorted Trees for years and never got beyond the theory because only a complete system can deliver real experience when applied to inner and outer situations. One cannot safely climb a ladder with many rungs missing. (Gate of Light, 16th century.)

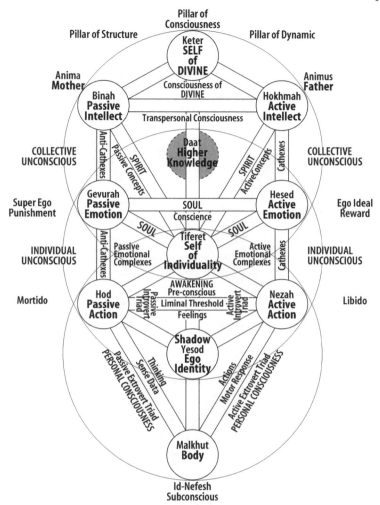

Figure 119—PSYCHE

Most of the time the body and its instincts take care of themselves. To a degree, the same is true of the lower mind. However, human evolution is contingent on conscious effort and some idea how the mind operates at different levels. This requires the Kabbalist to study the psyche in detail. Here we have the anatomy of what some call the 'astral' vehicle. It has a distinct structure and dynamic which is set out in ancient, medieval and modern terms. For example, the lower face is largely governed by the Nefesh *or vital life principle, called the Id by Freud. The soul in this scheme is the only triad that can apply free will, as the body dominates what is below it while the transpersonal part above is beyond in the unconscious.* (Halevi.)

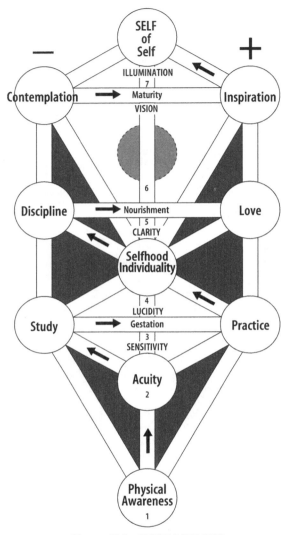

Figure 120—SEVEN STAGES
One of the first disciplines in Kabbalah is to be aware of the body which is governed by instinct. Level two is to alert the ordinary mind of the ego; and then the third stage of psychic sensibility. The fourth is to be lucidly awake to all going on. The fifth phase is to have a clarity of consciousness which can perceive the soul. Great artists and writers have this capacity. The sixth stage is to be able to see the transpersonal processes of history and the Spirit. The seventh state, at the Crown of the psyche, is to be simultaneously in contact with the place where the three upper worlds meet. (Halevi.)

a certain position in the Northern hemisphere. It has also been noted, over thousands of years, that people born in the winter tend to be introvert while the zodiacal position of the Moon appears to influence the character of the ego. The disposition of the planets has a similar effect on aspects of the psyche. A strong Venus, for example, seems to generate a sensual temperament while an afflicted Mars stimulates indecision.

The psyche, as can be seen in Figure 121, is half-embedded in the body. Where they interact is the domain of the *Nefesh* or instinctive mind. This is the 'Id' of Freud with its sexual drive and the libido and mortido principles, that is flight or fight, submission and aggression reflexes. In contrast, the soul triad of the Tree pivots on the Self of Tiferet that relates to Jung's view of individuation. It is here that the lower part of the psyche intermeshes with the upper section of the body. The result is that the psychological capacity to act, think and feel are greatly influenced by the senses and the state of the body. The ego or ordinary mind is more or less automatic, due to the demands of the body and the attitudes and habits acquired from the family and society. These are stored in the upper side triads as the Super Ego and Ego Ideal which manifest as the unconscious punishment and reward complexes that govern most people's lives.

The ancient and medieval Kabbalists did not know about the anatomy of the body in detail because dissection was forbidden but they did understand the levels present within. They saw the carnal organism in terms of the four elements; earth being its solids, water its fluidic processes with air as *Ruah*, the activating life principle. Fire was related to consciousness. The rabbis also recognised the mineral, vegetable and animal levels of intelligence within mankind and classified them according to an individual's conduct which rooted back to the ancient caste system of Israelite, Levite, Priest and High Priest. This was, at least, the theory as an Israelite might, like Rabbi Akiba, become a great scholar and mystic although he began life as a shepherd. In contrast a person could be born into a High Priest's family but descend, through corruption, into an animal state of seeking political power or, if only concerned with bodily appetites, become a vegetable level human. These things did happen. Remember the evil sons of priestly Eli who educated the prophet Samuel. They were lecherous and greedy and came to a bad end.

The psyche on the Tree is a very complex entity. However, everything is integrated and interacts through the sefirot, triads and

188

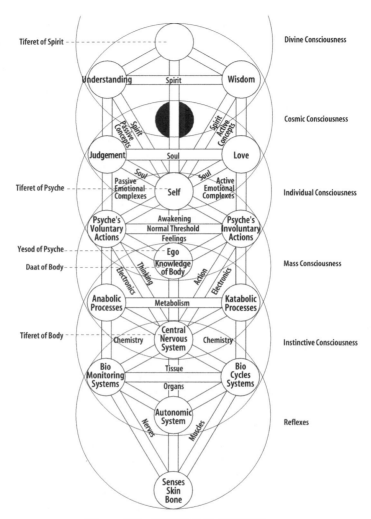

Figure 121 — BODY AND PSYCHE

In this scheme it is possible to see the interrelation between the mind and the physical vehicle. The meeting place is centred on the ego, under which lies the body's Daat or non-sefirah. This means that it is possible for the mind to imagine the state of the stomach. It also shows how events in, say, the feeling triad will resonate in its equivalent at the organ level. Hence negative feelings can manifest as heart- or head-ache. Likewise, if the left side of the psyche is inclined to depression, this will be seen in the body's tendency to tense the muscles and make body chemistry acidic. The converse is true in manic psyches that use up too much physical vitality. A balance of body and psyche is needed for any development. (Halevi.)

Figure 122—PSYCHISM
As the mind begins to awaken in the process of development, certain higher
centres of the brain and lower psyche start to operate. This opens the door to the
invisible realms. However, without training some people are overcome by
psychic phenomena because they cannot tell the difference between vision and
imagination; the voice of a discarnate maggid or a sub-persona of their own.
This is why it is necessary to have an experienced teacher and sane colleagues
who can monitor what is going on. This operation is like entering an astral jungle
where the psychological immune system can be breached, leading to possession.
(Rembrandt print, 17th century.)

Figure 123—STRUGGLE
The story of Jacob wrestling with an angel is not just a fable but a description of
a day-to-day situation. All spiritual traditions speak about the endless contest
between one's lower and higher natures. The body and lower psyche have strong
instincts and conditioning that seek to maintain a working routine. Any serious
change is a threat. The angel of the Self in bringing about a transformation has
to contain and control all the desires, habits and set ideas we all have. The fact
that this wrestling took place at night indicates Jacob was still psychologically
asleep. It was only at dawn, when he 'Awoke', that he was given the name Israel,
'He who struggles with and is the champion of God'. (Doré's Bible Illustrations,
19th century.)

paths. In general, the side pillars and triads are concerned with active and passive functions while those on the central column are associated with various degrees of consciousness. Body awareness is easy to identify; so, to a degree, is that of the ego. The feeling triad can be identified with unconscious psychic sensitivity, such as picking up others' moods, while the awakening triad is where we are particularly alert when we become aware of danger.

The triad of the soul is called by some Kabbalists the *Ruah* and by others the *Neshamah*. This is due to their definition in different periods and cultures. The Soul is the place of individual consciousness and choice. It is here that free will is exerted. However, this can only be exerted to the full when the individual has their psychological centre of gravity well established in this soul triad. For most people, the soul lies beyond the bio-psychological liminal line between Hod and Nezah, hidden in the unconscious.

The soul is composed of the paths between the triads of emotional complexes and the triads of concepts, to which it has access and by which it is influenced. The emotional triads contain all the personal experiences of pain and pleasure which evolve into a vast number of interconnected, strong and weak, memories. Some of these are easily accessible and some are not, for a number of reasons. They can range from lack of potency to strict repression. For example, one cannot remember people who are not memorable or one would rather forget. The triads concerned with concepts are, as noted, about the values of one's family, ethnic background and culture. The left-hand triad is about structure and restraint. For example, an orthodox Jew would never consider eating pork or think robbing a bank acceptable while their right-hand dynamic triad would consider giving to charity and devout prayer as obligatory. This is the power of cultural conditioning.

The great triad of Tiferet, Binah and Hokhmah is about the transpersonal spiritual dimension that is deep within the unconscious. For those who consider inner development, this is the Land of Milk and Honey. Like the ancient Israelites, they seek *Teshuvah*, to return to the place where they can enter the Heavenly Temple. Such a spiritual experience of this cosmic order is obtained through the agency of the psychological Hokhmah or Revelation, Binah or Reason and Daat, the veil before the Face of the Divine triad at the head of the Tree of the psyche. This has, through its Crown, direct contact with the bottom sefirah of the Highest Tree. Here is where the three upper worlds of

Formation, Creation and Emanation meet. Below, at the place of the Self, is where the Crown of the body, the Tiferet of the psyche and the Malkhut of spirituality come together. This means there are three aspects to the Self that ordinary psychology does not take into account. While this seems very complex, once the essential simplicity of the Tree and Jacob's Ladder has been absorbed, it is easy to comprehend the system. This is why the study of theory is important.

As can be seen from Figure 119, there are three circles or zones of general consciousness. That centred on the ego is mostly concerned with the routine of life where the ego acts as the psyche's servant. Unfortunately, it sometimes believes that it is the master of the psychological house. This rôle, in reality, belongs to the Self which is the pivot of the sphere of the individual's unconscious, in most people's cases. For the Kabbalist, the lesser state of Katnut belongs to the ego while the Gadlut or greater awareness awakens the Self and the soul. From here it is possible, with great effort, to attain an insight into the collective mind, the Spirit and the cosmic level of consciousness. Here is the place of prophecy and the gateway to the Divine.

This is the broad outline of the lower half of Jacob's Ladder. One may react intellectually or emotionally to its wondrous elegance. However, ironically, it is action that is required to make such knowledge real and part of one's life. It is not enough to read every book on Kabbalah or even practise some of its exercises. Nor is it enough, as one group did, to sing and chant texts they did not understand, believing this would enlighten. It is only by a commitment to applying increasing consciousness to the theory and practice that Kabbalah becomes real.

Kabbalah is about living life to the full within the limits of Divine Law, as set out in the Ten Commandments. Some people believe that the detailed regulations that have accumulated over the centuries are what Kabbalah is all about. These, in some cases, have become idols that have imprisoned many people and led to a rigid and crystallised form of the Tradition. As one rabbinic mystic observed, 'They see only the outer coat and not the inner soul which wears it'. The aim of Kabbalah is to aid God to behold God. Each of us is an organ of perception for the Holy One and so every situation and insight we consciously experience is of direct relevance, not only to the individual Self but the Godhead who is in the process, through us, of completing a SELF-portrait.

13. Practice

Within an ancient line like Kabbalah there are many different practices. Some are rooted in the Bible, others peculiar to their epoch and particular culture. One of the most well known Jewish religious rituals is *Pesach* or Passover. Here the family gathers at a time of year when other traditions celebrate the Spring. This is the point when the seemingly dead world of Winter revives again in an impulse of new life. As the Christian Easter corresponds to the pagan and heathen celebrations of the Earth god's resurrection, so Pesach represents the emergence of the Israelites out of the darkness of slavery. Here we see how archetypes are universal beneath their outer form.

During the Passover ceremony, those present are asked to consider themselves as actual Israelites at the event of Exodus. Indeed, some of the very old souls may well have been present there in previous lives, according to Kabbalah. As the ritual proceeds, various objects and actions represent the process of coming out from the Land of Bondage and the setting out for the Promised Land. While Pesach has an historic basis, behind it is the implication of freeing oneself from the imprisonment of physicality and entering into the desert zone of purification as the slave-minded generation dies off and a new, free one is born. At the end of the ceremony, in which four cups of wine represent the forty years journey ahead to climb the four levels of Jacob's Ladder, a door is opened for Elijah to appear, heralding the final Messiah and journey's end in Jerusalem. Most Jews are oblivious of the esoteric aspect of the ritual which largely became a traditional family ceremony, rather like the Christian Christmas when many relatives gather together.

Every day, Orthodox Jews put on what are called the *Tefilim*. These are ritual objects that are bound onto the arm in seven windings that terminate with three turns over the fingers while another box is strapped onto the head. The seven windings represent the lower sefirot and the three top ones, forming the Hebrew letter *Shin*, signify the Divine Name, SHADDAI, Almighty. These small leather boxes

Figure 124—ACTION
In this ceremony at the close of the Sabbath, a family acts out a tradition that has been carried on over the generations. Most rituals were designed to draw attention to the hidden realm in their symbolism. Unfortunately, over time the inner meaning is forgotten. The Kabbalist must either consider what such a traditional ritual once meant or invent a new one with spiritual content that awakens the soul to the Divine Presence in All. (Havdallah ceremony, 17th century.)

Figure 125—DEVOTION

An example of an unnoticed aspect of Jewish prayer is the swaying back and forth of the devotee. In an orthodox synagogue all the male congregants are seen to sway like a field of corn in the wind. This action is meant to represent a candle flame touched by Ruah Hakodesh, *the Holy Spirit or Wind of God. While this is going on the person is meant to say each word, knowing what it means and not just saying it by heart. This is called the* Gadlut *state in which the act of devotion is one of* Kavvanah: *conscious intention.* (A Jew at Prayer, Jewish Encyclopaedia, 20th century.)

Figure 126—CONTEMPLATION
This means much more than to just think about something. The Kabbalist takes
a concept or a story and considers it from every angle to gain a deeper and wider
insight into Existence. One exercise is the contemplation of the Sefirotic Tree;
another, what lies behind Joseph's ability to interpret dreams. These two could
be brought to reveal that Yesod, the sefirah of the Ego, is the psychic screen upon
which inner and outer conscious or unconscious images are projected. These
have to be interpreted by Tiferet, the Self, in physical, psychological or spiritual
terms, as Joseph did for Pharaoh, the symbol of the body. (Rabbi Akiba, 16th
century.)

contain an important text and are placed close to the heart and brain so as to remind the wearer that the Teaching should be absorbed by the soul and spirit. This daily ceremony should be carried out in the Gadlut state of being simultaneously conscious of the physical, emotional and intellectual levels.

There are many other small observances carried on in an orthodox home throughout the year to remind people, on both a personal and general scale, of the deeper and wider reality that lies beneath and above the everyday world. However, as often happens, these concepts and rituals can become mere religious routines. The aim of Kabbalah is to awaken practitioners to the hidden realities they symbolise.

To avoid forgetting what the Way of Action is meant to do, some Kabbalists constantly change or invent new ways to perform rituals. While traditionalists may object, it does keep the participant awake to what they are doing and not fall back into the state of mechanical routine or, in other words, 'slavery'. Another example is when Jews sway back and forth in prayer. Few know that this is symbolic of being within the Light of a Divine Flame which is present in everyone. Practising a custom without knowing its origin can lead to a form of sleep talking.

There was a rabbi who, after years of devotions in which nothing spiritual ever occurred, cried out in desperation, 'Lord, why dost Thou not respond to my words?' A still, small voice, deep within him replied, 'It is because you know not what you are saying'. Another example, but in reverse, was the story of the shepherd who said to God, everyday, that if the Almighty had sheep, he would take care of them for nothing. This was not the proper way to pray, according to a most learned rabbi, who happened to pass by one day. He stopped and taught the shepherd the correct form and moved on, very satisfied he had performed a good deed. That night, the rabbi was taken up, in a vivid dream, before the Throne of Heaven where he was told in no uncertain terms that the shepherd's simple sincerity was more real than all the priestly services in Jerusalem. He was to go back and tell the shepherd to return to his original prayer, as it was most pleasing to the Lord. It was a very humble rabbi who carried out his good deed for that day.

Another approach is seen in the answer when a rabbinic student was asked why he travelled so far to be taught by a particular teacher. He replied, 'To watch the way he ties up his boot laces'. While this may seem a facetious response, its implication is a key to a Kabbalistic

Figure 127—RELATIONSHIPS

In Kabbalah everything is a lesson. Marriage, for example, is one of the greatest initiations. It means a radical change of life. How does one relate to a person in a long-term and intimate situation? During courtship most people are on their best behaviour. After the honeymoon, a different reality takes over. Both individuals have to learn how to accommodate each other. This can awaken the best and worst in people. The Kabbalist sees this as an intensive learning situation. One rabbi, being asked how he could endure his shrewish wife, replied, "So who else would marry her?" (Jewish wedding, 19th century.)

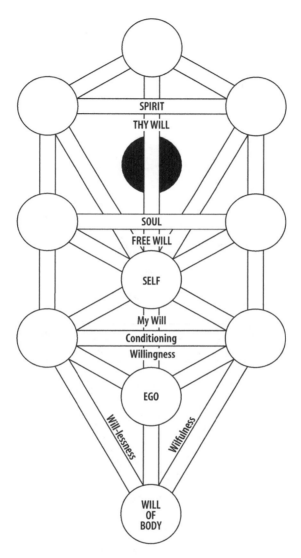

Figure 128—WILL
This is a crucial factor in Kabbalah. Without knowing the different wills at work within one there can be no progress. The will of the body is very powerful but easily identified. Not so with will-less-ness that allows people to get into difficult situations. The same is true of will-full-ness. The Kabbalist seeks to become willing. Then they can develop a conscious will that can control habitual reactions. Once established, then the person can submit at the level of the soul to the Divine. (Halevi.)

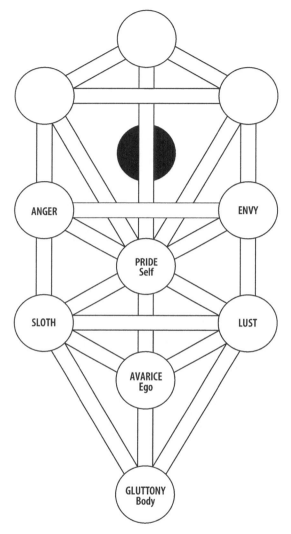

Figure 129—TEMPTATIONS
Here the seven deadly sins are clearly set out. Gluttony is related to the body; while Avarice is a problem of the ego that wishes to claim everything. Sloth is when the Mercurial aspect of body and mind is afflicted while Lust relates to an over-active Venusian function. Pride occurs when the Self is inflated by its sense of importance while Anger is the nasty side of discrimination and Envy the shadow aspect of generosity. Each vice will assault the Kabbalist at some point, to test his integrity. In the case of Esau, his hunger lost him the birthright of Isaac's spiritual inheritance. (Halevi.)

mode of studying the Teaching. The Way of Action means a corresponding development in the psyche and spirit. Most acts are not performed in the present but while the mind is elsewhere, in the past or future. A Master is in all three dimensions, even while he is tying his boots.

A more mundane practice is what Eastern European Jews of old called a 'Mensch'. This was a person who was fully human in their everyday activities. By this is meant to be true to one's nature and not just a cultivated personality such as being a professional saint or famous scholar. Advanced souls do not have to be learned or devout, although it helps. An example is the case of two travelling preachers. One visited a synagogue before and the other after a festival. The former gave an extremely erudite talk on the Torah and its symbolism, which greatly impressed the congregation, while the latter spoke about the Torah in everyday life. A month later most people could not remember a word of what the eloquent one had said but many things the other had spoken of were deeply engraved in their souls because he was a living example of what he talked about.

Jewish humour often contains the Teaching. This story reveals the difference between different levels of development.

A certain great scholar in old Tsarist Russia used give talks to remote Jewish communities as a religious duty. During one journey through the snow-bound countryside he sighed so deeply that his sleigh driver became quite concerned. Was there anything he could do, he asked his master. 'No! No!' replied the rabbi. 'I am just very weary and I have to give a lecture tonight on Kabbalah'. The driver then said, 'The people in the town we are going to do not know you. If we changed clothes, I could give your talk'. The rabbi was amazed and said, 'You are not a scholar and can hardly read or write. What do you know of such a subject?' The driver nodded and replied, 'True, but I have heard this particular lecture many times and I know it by heart.'

He then began to recite the rabbi's talk from beginning to end. 'Well?' said the coachman. 'Did I not even get your high points right?' 'Indeed', acknowledged the impressed rabbi, 'but what about the questions after the lecture?' The coachman shrugged and said, 'They always ask the same questions.' The rabbi laughed, nodded and agreed to change clothes, partly because he was desperately tired and also out of sheer curiosity as to what would happen. As they switched places, the coachman said 'I've always wanted to be a rabbi.'

(Above) Figure 130—BREAKTHROUGH
Kabbalah is about seeing behind appearances. Modern science has revealed worlds within worlds but a human being is a much finer and more powerful instrument than any microscope or telescope. The direct experience of the mystic can overcome time and space through the eye of vision and perceive the workings of Existence. Kabbalah has the techniques and metaphysical tools to make sense of what is seen. (16th century woodcut.)

(Right) Figure 131—EXERCISE
The ancient technique of guided imagination is still used to explore the higher worlds. Here an ordered progression of images takes the Kabbalist from the mundane world out of the body, up through an archetypal landscape to their maggid's house. From there they proceed to ascend in stages to the Heavenly Jerusalem where they glimpse the finest of Humanity, the angelics and the Temple of all Temples. Here, where the three upper realms meet, they may be permitted to see through the veil, view the Celestial Throne and experience the power of the Creator. This operation should be conducted by a senior teacher who then brings the student down to Earth and resets them in their body. (Halevi.)

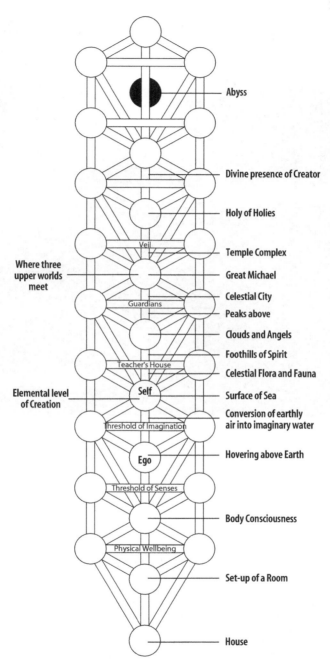

Abyss

Divine presence of Creator

Holy of Holies

Veil

Temple Complex

Where three
upper worlds
meet

Great Michael

Celestial City

Guardians

Peaks above

Clouds and Angels

Foothills of Spirit

Teacher's House

Celestial Flora and Fauna

Self

Surface of Sea

Elemental level
of Creation

Conversion of earthly
air into imaginary water

Threshold of Imagination

Ego

Hovering above Earth

Threshold of Senses

Body Consciousness

Physical Wellbeing

Set-up of a Room

House

Figure 132—HALLS OF RECORDS
One of the levels encountered during an inner ascent is that of the Heavenly Paradise. Here are the Academies on High, a kind of celestial university where all human achievement, including the records of every historical event, are kept. Old and new lost works of art, science, philosophy and religion are to be found here. So too are various masters who act as tutors to anyone who comes and wishes to develop. This is the place where the Maggidim are trained, in order to guide those seekers who still walk the Earth. (John Martin, 19th century.)

When they arrived in the town the rabbi, in his driver's gear, sat at the back of the synagogue and listened to his coachman expound on the mysteries of Creation, mankind and God. The driver, in his rabbinic costume, was convincing as he knew his lines and skilfully applied all his master's intonations and gestures. When he was given a standing ovation by the congregation, he looked across to the rabbi and smiled. See—he, too, could be admired as a man of great learning. Then came the questions which were the usual ones, as predicted. The driver gave all the standard answers with, perhaps, a certain flourish at his triumph. However, someone in the mesmerised congregation, seeking a deeper explanation, came up with a question that had never been asked before. The driver became speechless. He had no idea what to say as he did not even understand what was being asked. After some silence, in which the congregation waited expectantly for his wisdom, he suddenly blurted out, 'This is such a stupid question, ask my coachman.'

This story illustrates the difference between a well-conditioned ego and a long and deeply experienced Self. On the Tree of the psyche, here is Yesod assuming the role of Tiferet. This is the case for most people of the vegetable level who are governed and controlled by their instincts and cultural habits and attributes. Animal level people are halfway between the ego and the Self, as they have moments when they are aware of more than the physical and the obvious. This is why some business people are so successful. They are like predators on the hunt, on the lookout for a profitable deal.

The rabbi was of a different order. He was visiting these remote communities not to make a living, as some did, but because it was his vocation. He took on such a mission because someone had to sow seeds of Kabbalah in distant places for those who were ready to start their development. This was his work and destiny. Such individuals are to be found all over the world in every spiritual tradition. Their hallmark is a profound seriousness and yet laced with light but loaded humour.

There are seven levels within the psyche, known as the seven lower halls. The first four are concerned with the body and lower psyche; the fifth level is that of the soul which perceives life as a whole and not just a current situation. The soul has memories of other previous lives and places where it has been. This manifests in a seemingly irrational attraction or repulsion as regards different people, countries and periods. However, while this is of great interest at some stage in

Figure 133—MARKET PLACE
While the Kabbalist may explore the invisible realms, the ordinary world must not be forgotten. The everyday world is where the greatest progress can be made because here all the possibilities are present. This is because the Earthly contains the physical, psychological, spiritual and Divine dimensions whereas the Higher Worlds lack material substance. On Earth every situation is a potential step along the Path. Even while in the market place, something important can be learnt. As one rabbi observed, 'Everything has its purpose, each moment is an opportunity'. (Market day in old Russia, 19th century engraving.)

one's development, the present is much more important. This is where we are learning our current life's lesson.

If one has worked inwardly enough to have karmically earned the fate to encounter and enter a school of the soul, other students, as well as one's teacher, will help in development. These are real friends who have trodden a similar path and know what it is about to go through, for example, a transformational crisis. These sometimes very tough situations are vital for personal evolution, otherwise stagnation will occur. A pleasant and uneventful period, for example, can be very seductive and cause one to become complacent, whereas a difficult challenge can make one expand beyond present limits. It is at such a time that one's esoteric colleagues can be a great support when one's family have no idea of what is going on.

As regards very hard times, the question should be 'Why is this happening?' It may be the result of some old karma or discarded redundant patterns or something more recent that needs immediate attention. The Kabbalist must be scrupulously honest; moreover, their spiritual companions must not shirk from pointing out what might be the cause of such suffering. However, they must be very sensitive and tactful in how they deal with the problem. Those are very practical operations, although they may be concerned with psychological or spiritual issues. One's blood kin family often cannot comprehend such crises as they are often part of the problem. It is wise, therefore, if one wishes to develop, to marry someone on the 'Path' so that both can understand what is going on and give each other real support.

This brings up the recurring question about soul mates. According to tradition, they can only meet when they are psychologically mature enough to work on the personal and transpersonal levels. A negative example of two soul mates, who were not ready to come together, was the fact that they became totally obsessed with each other; the result was that they were useless as far as anybody else and the Universe was concerned. The sheer intensity of their relationship eventually broke them up before they burnt each other out. Most of us have to practise being in a sound working relationship with people very close to us in development until we are mature enough at every level to be able to make a real marriage. Then the soul mate will appear. However, it may not mean the wedding, home and children type. It can be a professional, social or esoteric partnership. The fullest marriage is made in Heaven.

Practice makes perfect. This, however, is not about attaining a mechanical efficiency but raising consciousness up beyond the body and mind to the wider dimensions of where we, as individuals and collectively, fit into the cosmic scheme and Divine Plan. It is only by moment to moment, day to day and year to year practice and observation that one can gain insight and then vision into what our personal and general task is, in the period we live in. Of equal importance is the awareness of evil that tests our integrity, especially in the subtleties of psychological Self-deception and Spiritual delusion by which the Lucific principle opposes Evolution.

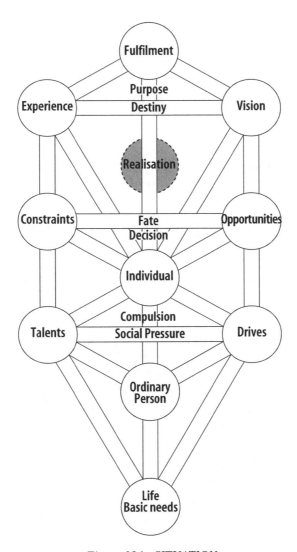

Figure 134—SITUATION
Here is what faces everyone on Earth, no matter where they are. First, all have to meet their basic needs, then learn how to work within their family and local society. Many stagnate at this vegetable level. Those who go on to become animal people exploit their talents to the full because they have a strong compulsive drive. Those who want to individuate have to choose between what is and is not possible. Over time they come to know, through reflection and revelation, what their particular mission is. This brings them Self realisation and fulfilment. (Halevi.)

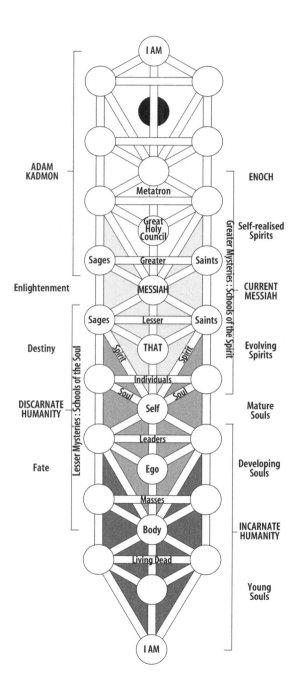

14. Realisation

The endless battle between good and evil is recognised by most esoteric traditions. It can take place at the level of a nation or an individual. Tradition says we live with a devil on one shoulder and an angel on the other. Both make suggestions and give us advice but it is our choice as to what we do. These two archetypes represent the shadow and the light within our personal being and at work inside a society.

The Bible is full of stories of this struggle; so too is history where rulers and peoples actively or passively precipitate creative or destructive events. The law of measure for measure or karma results in retribution. This term does not only mean 'an eye for an eye' but also reward. Solomon was given wealth and power, as well as wisdom, because he asked to be able to govern well. Alas, legends tell how he went mad for a while when he thought he could outwit Asmodeus, the Evil One. This was a harsh lesson.

Indeed, both hard and easy lessons are the basis of human evolution. The plant and animal kingdoms take millions of years to develop because they are not conscious of being conscious and are subject to general terrestrial and celestial conditions. Humanity, however, is not totally under the domain of general laws. Because of this, mankind has progressed very rapidly over the last few millennia. This brings in the factor of the *Gilgulim*, the process of reincarnation, which allows experience gained to be passed on as the psyche is immortal. Along with the accumulated knowledge recorded and developed by civilisation, mankind's progress has rapidly accelerated.

(Left) Figure 135—PRESENT
At this point in history, most of humanity is still undeveloped. The world is still a nursery for these young souls. The leaders of any society are usually animal people while those seeking to be fully human are graduated according to their level. They are the spearhead of incarnate humanity. Above them comes the Messiah at that point in time. He or she co-ordinates with the higher saints, sages and mystics to oversee the evolution of mankind. The Living Dead are those who have suppressed their consciences or destroyed their chance to develop in their present incarnation. (Halevi.)

Figure 136—PROPHECY
Here a student with his maggid views the wheels of Life and Death as they spiral up from the Earth or descend to begin another life. To see on this scale is to perceive history in a prophetic way. Most of recorded history is about violence, winners and losers, but the reality is that only those who contribute positively to human development are worth remembering. The most obvious are the great teachers, who generate civilisations, but inventors, explorers and even great merchants as well as artists, scientists and poets have their place in the real history of the world. (Doré's illustration for Dante's *Divine Comedy,* 19th century.)

Figure 137—FINAL JOURNEY
Here Moses is seen leading the Israelites out of Egypt. He represents the inner Teacher. Behind him come our slave-minded sub-personalities. They are about to cross the Red Sea of commitment and face many trials of development before they reach the Land of Enlightenment. Out of the undisciplined tribes will emerge a nation or integrated psyche. It is a long but worthwhile journey, much better than living as a slave or wandering endlessly about in the wilderness of uncertainty.
(Haggadah, 19th century.)

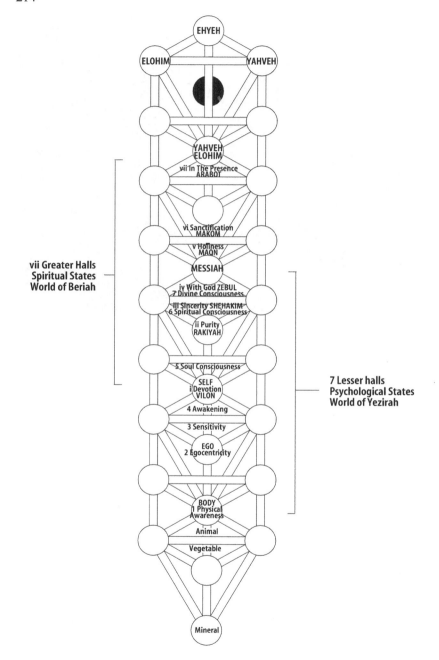

EHYEH

ELOHIM YAHVEH

YAHVEH
ELOHIM
vii In The Presence
ARABOT

vi Sanctification
MAKOM

v Holiness
MAON

MESSIAH

iv With God ZEBUL
7 Divine Consciousness

iii Sincerity SHEHAKIM
6 Spiritual Consciousness

ii Purity
RAKIYAH

5 Soul Consciousness

SELF
i Devotion
VILON

4 Awakening

3 Sensitivity

EGO
2 Egocentricity

BODY
1 Physical
Awareness

Animal

Vegetable

Mineral

vii Greater Halls
Spiritual States
World of Beriah

7 Lesser halls
Psychological States
World of Yezirah

Each day a million or so souls pass through the gates of birth and death. However, the option to progress or regress, the gift of Free Will, is in the hands of each person to exercise or not. As every life, according to Kabbalah and other esoteric traditions, is designed according to karma, so exactly the right conditions are presented. These may be easy or difficult. This explains many seemingly unjust fates where the good suffer and the bad prosper. However, there is more to it than appearances.

A lifetime is but a day within a long chain of incarnations in which the universal law of equilibrium is worked out. For example, while evil leaders are often blamed, for instance, for massacres, it is often quite ordinary people who carry them out. Important war criminals are tried and executed but how else can the average person who participates in such crimes of passion be called to account, except by being born to suffer what they had done to others?

The answer is that they are reborn in a situation in which they will experience what they inflicted on others. The same is true for individual murderers, adulterers and many other misdemeanours. As can be seen in life, there is no shortage of people to commit criminal or immoral acts and so there is a continuous leapfrog of bad karma, until a person or society realises that there is no benefit from 'missing the mark'. Europe had to have two disastrous wars in order to perceive that nationalism is very destructive. Out of this came the European Union. It is the same on a personal level when an individual recognises that there is no profit in evil.

Kabbalah sees history as a 'passing show' but one in which much can be learnt. Indeed, this is the purpose of life on Earth, the World of Action, where all that exists is concentrated at every level. Originally matter only existed in a primitive solid, liquid, gaseous and radiant form but now the planet has a great pyramid of metals, minerals and

Figure 138—MAP
This Jacob's Ladder marks out each rung of the journey. All the stages have to be gone through. If one is missed or avoided then, in the esoteric game of Snakes and Ladders, any sin—which means 'to miss the mark' in Hebrew—results in sliding down so as to face the test again. The lower levels are relatively easy to recognise but the higher ones are increasingly subtle. As one master noted, 'What can a frog know of the ocean?' The Worlds beyond the psyche have no forms and so we have to go by the symbols the mystics have given to us as a guide. The four upper levels can be defined as Touching the Divine, being in the place of Holiness, hearing the Archangels at prayer and coming into the Presence of the CREATOR. (Traditional scheme, Halevi.)

Figure 139—ICON
This word means a sacred image that is a door into the unseen realms. Here the Heavenly Jerusalem is where the three higher Worlds meet. It is the epitome of high civilisation. Its inhabitants are those who have reached the level where they can be great mystics, sages and saints or masters in their particular fields. These include the so-called humble occupations. A peasant is sometimes wiser than a university professor. In this engraving, the Light from the Divine Realm shines down, indicating there are yet higher stages above. Here the winged Teacher, indicating they can rise up, instructs the student, still relatively Earth-bound. (Doré's Bible Illustrations, 19th century.)

Figure 140—ANOINTED

In the Sufi mystical tradition this living person is called the Axis of the Age. They might also be considered the Buddha of their time. At this level, local culture is not relevant as the position can only be held by one who has gone beyond it. However, they must also be worldly wise, as this position of head of the Earthly spiritual hierarchy requires it. Historically, it is quite a dangerous role as it is a direct threat to the religious or political establishment. Therefore only a few in the chain of Messiahs are known. One was King David, another Zoroaster and yet another the Buddha. (16th century print.)

218

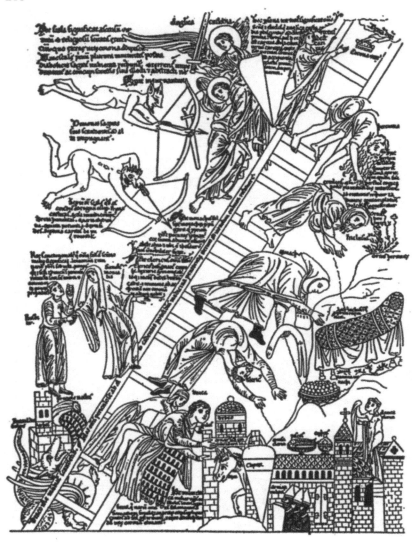

Figure 141—OPPOSITION
Lucifer attempts to stop every aspirant from evolving. This can occur in any situation, from a trivial quarrel to a cosmic issue. The Lucific test can manifest from either the shadow or Light side of a situation or from deep within a person. One Kabbalistic tradition says that we have an angel on one shoulder and a devil on the other. However, the choice is ours as to whom we listen. Here, devils wait in the outer darkness of the Kellippot, ready to tempt susceptible climbers. (Medieval manuscript.)

organic life. Humanity is adding the psychological and spiritual dimensions through its personal and general evolution. Conversely, mankind can damage the planet by its carelessness and create a bad negative karma for its own future incarnations.

Within mankind, about ninety percent operate at the vegetable level with around nine percent in the animal level. Roughly one percent of the world's population has reached the level of being fully human. Within this, as Figure 135 shows, are various degrees of evolution. The most advanced are usually concentrated in the cities and towns of each nation but many are to be found in the countryside as local wise folk or Shamans. These are old souls who are also found to be operational in slums, war zones and even in the military.

Providence is the mechanism that oversees and organises such placings, like the director of a drama in which each actor has their place in the plot and must learn their lines well before being allowed to do a bigger part. Providence is run by what is called the Higher Circle, the Companions or Blessed Company who, in turn, are watched over by the Great Holy Council, headed by Enoch. Members of this spiritual elite would include all the greatest of Spiritual Teachers.

It is this stratum of history that generates change. Most leaders in every walk of life who believe they make the world go round are deluded. Their words and works soon fade away. They are only remembered because of scholars who often write a distorted account of what happened, according to whether they are winners or losers. However, great teachers' works and many other unworldly achievements are still alive with us because they contain eternal truths. The Bible is a classic example; Plato is still read and Buddha's words are still heard.

Why is this so? The reason is because deep in every human being is a microcosm of Existence which resonates with the universal principles. Take, for example, the rabbinic saying, 'Do as you would be done by.' This phrase is found in every genuine spiritual tradition. It is the beginning of the realisation that every human is as oneself. Moreover, that Self is the same for everyone. A Kabbalist was once walking through the street of a great city when he saw, in every face, the countenance of the Divine beneath whatever expression was on the faces of the thousands of persons seen.

Here to be witnessed was I AM within not only the living but those passing out of and into life. Death does not kill the Divine which will

Figure 142—SPIRITUAL REALM
Here the aspirant, moving through the world of celestial Air, approaches the fiery Gate of the Divine. According to a Kabbalistic account, when four rabbis reached this level, one died; one went mad; another rejected what he experienced. The last, a mystic who had been well trained, did not lose his nerve and survived the awesome sight. This story is a warning to those who are not disciplined but seek, in a sense, illegally to enter the higher levels of Existence. (John Martin, 19th century.)

take on a new body in the next incarnation, after a period of reflection in between lives. Life on Earth is where all the levels are to be found and where they can interact. In the realms beyond physicality they are normally separated. No criminal is found in Paradise, nor is any good soul to be seen in Hell. It is only in the lowest world of incarnation that all the levels meet. The reason is that here the situation is like a pressure cooker or place where there is every opportunity for growth.

There are those souls who swim wilfully against the tide or willingly drift into degradation. These can become the Living Dead who, for this life, destroy their possibilities and sink down into an incarnate Hell until it is so unbearable that, in their next life, they decide not to follow the path of evil. A number of great saints came from this Lucific school of the soul. Even the Devil has its purpose.

On the positive side, the vast majority of humanity is slowly evolving. While there are still areas of savagery in the world, most people are better off and informed about global events and seeking a higher standard of life. Many, once doomed to ignorance and poverty, now want further education, to travel and widen their horizons. International communication is dissolving distance and ignorance about other cultures. Individuation is becoming more common. This is the beginning of a new epoch.

The Kabbalists and other esoteric communities can now be directly in touch with each other and enhance the universal and perennial Teaching. The author has spoken with a Native American medicine man, for example, who said that their version of Jacob's Ladder was circular. He has also talked with a Shinto Priest who recognised and acknowledged a fellow Companion of the Light. Conversations with Moslem, Sufi and Christian mystics have revealed just how much they have in common. Kabbalists throughout history have always moved with the times which is why the Tradition never died and the Work continues.

222

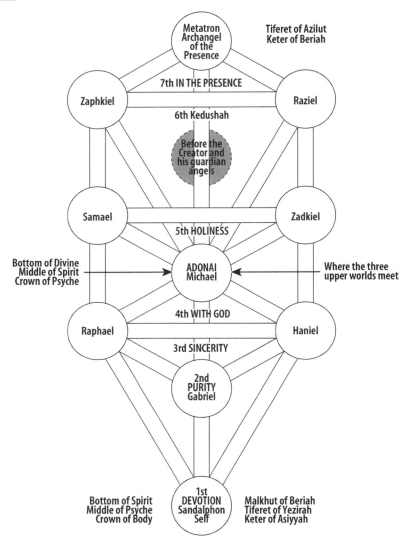

Figure 143—HOLY MOUNTAIN
This has to be climbed in measured stages. Each level requires an ability to maintain balance without being swept away by powerful cosmic forces. Devotion holds one steady, purity protects by being centred while sincerity keeps the aim on target. This is to gain access to where the three upper Worlds meet. If one is permitted to go beyond, there is assistance from the senior saints and sages and even from members of the Great Holy Council; and in rare cases, Metatron. (Halevi.)

15. *Return*

Before the Fourth and last journey of humanity, when it has completed its task of Self-realisation, a great deal has to happen. Evolution is a process that is vast and long in scale. Unlike the other three journeys, this final ascent is the return of the whole of mankind to the Absolute in the echo of the second utterance of I AM at the End of Days.

At this moment in history we have, in the 21st century of the Common Era, war, famine and plague—all the symptoms of a collective disorder. The human race, at the higher levels, has made great advances in development but, at the middle and lower strata, little has changed since prehistoric times. This is due to the power struggles at the personal, political and economic animal level and the subjection of the vegetable level who have been fed, since Roman times, a diet of bread and circuses and later a carrot and stick by church and state in the offers of salvation and glory through submission and sacrifice. Millions believed and followed. These false promises were meant to provide a permanent security that was never fulfilled. In medieval times it was religion and, in the modern Age of social revolution, political systems. Neither delivered peace or equality to the masses.

Today we have a confrontation between the extremes of soulless materialism and sectarian fanaticism that could bring about Armageddon. The choice, a current mystic observed, is that humanity has to choose between delusion and reality, destruction or progression. One does not have to be an Old Testament prophet to foresee a potential disaster if the omens are disregarded. While this is a gloomy possibility, those with a real and deep understanding of what is happening are working to offset the imbalance before the tipping point is reached. This is the responsibility of the esoteric community, of which the Kabbalistic Tradition is part.

Scattered around the world are many old and wise souls. Their task, openly or discreetly, is to educate and influence humanity at every level. There are those who, for example, work among ordinary people, to take them beyond the tribal and national view and perceive

Figure 144—DOOR TO THE DIVINE
Here the aspirant and his maggid guide view the archangelics calling to each
other, Kaddosh! Kaddosh! Kaddosh! *Holy! Holy! Holy! None, however, are*
permitted to enter into the world of the Sefirot; only human beings are allowed
in. It was from here that Enoch, the first fully SELF-realised person, went
through the Gate of Light into the HOLY PRESENCE and was transformed into
the illuminated being Metatron who became the Prince of the World and final
Messiah when the End of Days began. (Doré illustration for Dante's *Divine*
Comedy, 19th century.)

Figure 145—IMAGE OF GOD
Isaiah the prophet saw this vision in the Temple. It was but a radiant impression
of Adam Kadmon but it left an indelible experience that Kabbalists seek ultimately
to emulate. It is said that if this state is attained, then the ordinary everyday
world would appear to be shot through with Divine Light. Moreover, all would
be seen as a living process of Evolution, be it a stone, a flower or flock of birds.
Every personal incident or general event would be seen as part of a Divine Plan,
even the seemingly fixed stars would be observed to move according to the music
of the celestial spheres. Here Adam Kadmon, the perfection of Existence, is the
instrument by which the Absolute might be indirectly seen. (Rev. Kirby's Bible,
20th century.)

Figure 146—I AM THAT I AM
This rendering, in flaming Hebrew letters, of EHYEH ASHER EHYEH is the key
to All. It is the Absolute stating the highest Holy Name and intention. The first
WORD was given to Moses on Mount Sinai as to WHO was addressing him, then
came 'That' which related the first to the second 'I AM'. Here was the reason
for Existence in that this Holy set of Names was the source and echo that
reflected the origin of All, so that God could behold God in the micro- and
macrocosm of Existence. (Calligraphy by Prof James Russell.)

humanity as a whole, a family. The United Nations, at its best, performs this function because one of its early Secretary Generals was involved with the esoteric dimension and was well aware of the larger picture. Others on the Path operate within government, commerce and the arts and sciences, quietly influencing politics, economics and global culture. Evidence of this is seen in various international projects concerned with health, global warming and space.

At the more personal level, individuals trained in an esoteric understanding of hidden processes behind history help, advise and heal millions of people in every walk of life. They are generally unobtrusive and operate within every society, large or small. They are what one great master called 'The salt of the Earth'. Their task is to aid the transformation of mankind so that it comes to appreciate the Divine Work of Art being created, formed and made all around it. New technology has allowed us to glimpse the atom and penetrate deep space. The best of the media reveal, amid a plethora of sex, violence and vulgarity, images of beauty and profundity.

These vital 'other' contributions by old and mature souls, guided by spiritual teachers both incarnate and discarnate, may help avert disaster like the two World Wars, the Black Death and several seemingly natural devastations that had their origins in negative collective karma such as nationalism, corruption and exploitation.

Meanwhile, the Work goes on in Kabbalah and other esoteric schools to help those wishing inwardly to develop and become the ever-increasing segment of the conscious element in humanity. One by one, individuals cross the line between those who sleepwalk through life and those who step off the wheels of repetitive reincarnation. These climb Jacob's Ladder but participate in the cosmic operation of working harmoniously with creation and attracting others to fulfil their full potential. Every human being has a destiny. This was instilled in the Divine Spark that is present in everyone. Depending upon which part of Adam Kadmon we come from, each person must discover their particular function. This is the aim of Kabbalah, so that each may serve the Holy One and aid God to behold God.

As regards the ultimate return to the Absolute this, according to prophecy, will be the moment when humanity has done all it can do in the present cosmic cycle. Then, it is said, the last Messiah, Enoch, will appear on Earth after the Evil of mankind has been confronted, prior to a Golden Age in this, the lowest of the Worlds. Then, it is foretold, at its high point humanity will be taken up Jacob's Ladder

for the Final Judgement or assessment with all the creatures as regards their performance.

When this is done, humanity will rise and return, each to their own sacred place within the body of Adam Kadmon, bringing the experience of myriads of lifetimes and consciousness of every world into the awareness of a composite and unified SELF. This will complete the ultimate SELF-portrait as the great curtain hung down from Heaven will be drawn up into the Divine Realm. Time will then cease as the passing show and the Eternal Now become one. In that moment Adam Kadmon's eyes will open and realise, in the act of reflection, that I AM is the image of I AM. Then 'Face will gaze upon Face'. After this, tradition says, all will dissolve back into NO-THING-NESS again before, perhaps, beginning another great and more perfect cycle.

Spring 2006/5766
London

Figure 147 (Left)— WORK OF THE KABBALIST
Here the aspirant lives within the elemental world and relates to plants and animals as well as the physical universe. However, they are also conscious of the Worlds of Formation and Creation where Great Michael commands the Heavenly Hosts. Above, Metatron watches over the central column of human development and converses with the Divine Realm. Kabbalah is sometimes called the Work of Unification; that is, bringing about a connection between all the worlds, thus becoming the perfect SELF-portrait of the Absolute in miniature. (Halevi.)

Glossary of Kabbalistic Terms

ARABOT	Seventh heaven.
ASIYYAH	The World of making, of elements and action.
AYIN	Absolute No-thing.
AZILUT	The World of Emanation. The Divine realm of Adam Kadmon. The Glory.
BARAKAH	Blessing or Grace.
BERIAH	The World of Creation, pure Spirit and archangels.
BINAH	Sefirah of Understanding. Head of passive column. Great Mother.
DAAT	Unmanifest sefirah of Knowledge on central column.
EGO	Yesod of Yezirah. Ordinary consciousness.
EN SOF	Absolute All, or the Infinite without End.
GADLUT	The major conscious state.
GEHINNOM	Hell, Kellippot or the Pit.
GEVURAH	Sefirah of Judgement on the passive column.
GILGULIM	Transmigration of souls or rebirth.
HAIOT HAKODESH	Four Holy Living Creatures—Man, Eagle, Lion and Bull—at Keter of Yezirah.
HASID	A pious man, a saint of Hesed.
HESED	Sefirah of Mercy on active column.
HOD	Reverberation.Sefirah at base of passive pillar.
HOKHMAH	Sefirah of Wisdom at head of Active pillar. Great Father.
JUBILEE	End of a Great Cosmic Cycle.
KATNUT	The lesser conscious state.
KAVVANAH	Prayer with conscious intention.
KELLIPPOT	World of Shells, demons and disorder.
KETER	The Crown. Sefirah at head of central pillar of Equilibrium.
LOWER FACE	Figure described on any Tree by Malkhut-Hod-Tiferet-Nezah and Yesod.

MAGGIDIM	Spiritual Teachers.
MALKHUT	The Kingdom. Lowest sefirah on Tree.
MENORAH	Seven-branched candlestick of Moses.
MERKABAH	Chariot, or Yeziratic World of Psyche.
MESSIAH	The Anointed One. Axis of Age.
METATRON	Archangel of Presence at Keter of Beriah. The transfigured Enoch's title.
NEFESH	Animal or vital soul.
NESHAMAH	Human soul.
NEZAH	Eternity. Sefirah at base of active pillar.
RUAH	Spirit.
SANDALPHON	Enoch's title at Malkhut of Beriah.
SELF	Tiferet of Yezirah. One's inner guide.
SEFIROT	Containers, numbers, lights of the Attributes of God on the Tree. Singular: sefirah.
SHEKHINAH located	The Presence of God. The Bride in exile in Malkhut of Azilut.
SHEMITTAH	Great Year or Cosmic Cycle.
SHETIYAH	Foundation Stone of the World. Jacob's Pillow.
TALMUD	Recorded commentaries on the Bible and Oral Tradition.
TESHUVAH	Redemption or Conversion.
TIFERET	Central sefirah called Beauty. Meeting place of upper and lower faces.
TIKUNE	Conscious amendment to cosmic imbalances.
UPPER FACE Keter-	Figure described on Tree by Tiferet-Binah-Hokhmah and Daat.
YESOD Ego-	Foundation. Sefirah in middle of lower face. mind in psyche.
YEZIRAH	World of Formation. Psychological realm in man. World of Angels.
ZADEK Yesod	The just and righteous man associated with and Tiferet path.
ZAHZAHOT	The Three Hidden Lights in the Godhead.
ZELEM	An image.
ZIMZUM	The Contraction within the Godhead to allow existence to come into being.

Index